Table of Contents

Introduction

The Stories

Types of Stories

- fairy tales
- fables
- tall tales
- realistic fiction
- nonfiction
- poetry

Ways to Use the Stories

1. Directed lessons
   - with small groups of students reading at the same level
   - with an individual student

2. Partner reading

3. With cooperative learning groups

4. Independent practice
   - at school
   - at home

Things to Consider

1. Determine your purpose for selecting a story—instructional device, partner reading, group work, or independent reading. Each purpose calls for a different degree of story difficulty.

2. A single story may be used for more than one purpose. You might first use the story as an instructional tool, have partners read the story a second time for greater fluency, and then use the story at a later time for independent reading.

3. When presenting a story to a group or an individual for the first time, review any vocabulary that will be difficult to decode or understand. Many students will benefit from a review of the vocabulary page and the questions before they read the story.

Types of Skill Pages

Five pages of activities covering a variety of reading skills follow each story:

- comprehension
- vocabulary
- phonics
- structural analysis
- parts of speech
- record information

Ways to Use the Skill Pages

1. Individualize skill practice for each student with tasks that are appropriate for his or her needs.

2. As directed minilessons, the skill pages may be used in several ways:
   - Make a transparency for students to follow as you work through the lesson.
   - Write the activity on the board and call on students to fill in the answers.
   - Reproduce the page for everyone to use as you direct the lesson.

3. When using the skill pages for independent practice, make sure that the skills have been introduced to the reader. Review the directions and check for understanding. Review the completed lesson with the student to determine if further practice is needed.

Fun in the Snow

"It's snowing! It's snowing!" shouted Jay and Joy. The children were so excited they couldn't sit still. They ran around the house, yelling and jumping up and down.

"Children, settle down," called Mother. "You're too noisy for indoors. Why don't you get dressed and go outside and play for a while?"

The children …

tugged on their snow boots,
zipped up their warm jackets,
put on their furry earmuffs,
pulled on their wool gloves,
and wrapped striped scarves
around their necks.

Now they were ready to go outside and play in the snow.

Jay built a row of funny little snowmen. Joy plopped down in the snow and moved her arms back and forth to make snow angels. Then they made a huge pile of snowballs and had a snowball fight. The children laughed and played all afternoon.

Suddenly the children heard bells ringing. They looked up to see a large gray horse pulling a red and blue sleigh. They saw that Grandpa was driving the sleigh.

The horse and sleigh stopped in front of the house. "Does anyone here want a sleigh ride?" asked Grandpa.

"I do!" shouted Jay.
"Me, too!" laughed Joy.

Just then Mother came out. "Wait for me!" she called. "I want to go for a sleigh ride, too!"

Mother and the children hopped onto the sleigh. Away they rode as it began to snow again.

Name _____

Questions about *Fun in the Snow*

1. Why did Mother send the children outdoors?

   _____

2. What did the children put on to go out in the snow?

   _____

3. On what part of your body do you wear these things?

   a scarf   _____

   earmuffs   _____

4. Name three ways Jay and Joy played in the snow.

   _____

   _____

5. Who went for a sleigh ride?

   _____

6. How do you know it was a very cold day?

   _____

Think about It

What would you do on a snowy day?

_____

_____

Name _____

What Does It Mean?

Write each word after its meaning.

earmuffs   sleigh   wool
scarf   suddenly   wrap

1. a piece of cloth worn around the neck or head   _____

2. to put an outer covering around   _____

3. a type of cloth made from the hair of a sheep   _____

4. covers to protect ears from the cold   _____

5. a large vehicle with runners used on snow   _____

Tell what each phrase means.

settle down   _____

all bundled up   _____

What Is It?

Use words from the
story to label the picture.

1 _____

2 _____

3 _____

4 _____

5 _____

Name _____

Spell Long *a*

a–e	ay	ai	eigh
name	stay	stain	eight

Write the missing letters on the lines.

snowfl____k____

sl_____

p_____nt

c____k____

r_____n

_____t

Same–Opposite

Circle the pairs of words that are opposites.
Make an **X** on the pairs of words that mean the same.

up–down   happy–jolly

large–big   play–work

fast–speedy   tiny–little

noisy–quiet   front–back

indoors–outside night–day

Name _____

Pronouns

<table>
<tr><td>she</td><td>he</td><td>I</td><td>we</td><td>they</td><td>it</td></tr>
<tr><td>her</td><td>him</td><td>me</td><td>us</td><td>them</td><td></td></tr>
</table>

Write a pronoun for each noun that is underlined.

1. The children ran around the house.   _____

2. A gray horse pulled the sleigh.   _____

3. Grandpa asked, "Does anyone want a ride?"   _____

4. Jay and I like to play in the snow.   _____

5. Grandpa waited for Mother.   _____

6. Mother made hot chocolate for Jay and Joy.   _____

Past and Present

The words below are in the present tense. They tell what happens now. Write the past tense of each word. Make the word tell what already happened.

1. shout _____   4. eat   _____

2. run   _____   5. begin _____

3. play   _____   6. make   _____

Use the proper tense to fill in the blanks.

1. The children _____ in the snow all afternoon.

2. Mother will _____ hot chocolate for the children.

3. It _____ to snow again.

Name _____

Add a Suffix

Add **ing** and **ed** to each word.

1. play _____ _____

2. paint _____ _____

3. pull _____ _____

Double the last letter and add **ing** and **ed**.

1. tug _____ _____

2. zip _____ _____

3. wrap _____ _____

Drop the **e** and add **ing**.

1. move _____

2. excite _____

3. smile _____

Just add **d**.

1. move _____

2. excite _____

3. smile _____

Write sentences using one word from each section.

1. _____

2. _____

3. _____

4. _____

The Mystery of the Missing Blue Shoe

Rama was very happy. She had a brand new pair of shoes. Her shoes were blue with silver buckles just like she had wanted. She set the shoes on the floor by the foot of her bed. She could not wait to wear them to school.

The next morning, Rama jumped out of bed. She pulled on her socks and went to get her shoes. The shoe for her left foot was right where she had put it. "Where is my other shoe?" she said. Rama looked under the bed. She found an old boot. She found three socks. She found her dog's toy bone. But there was no blue shoe.

Rama looked all over the bedroom. She couldn't find the missing shoe. "This is a mystery," she said. "Where can that shoe be?"

Rama sat down to think about her problem. Maybe her little sister had taken the shoe. She liked to walk around in Rama's shoes. No, she would have taken two shoes, not one.

Had her brother taken the shoe? No, he stayed at a friend's house last night. He couldn't have taken it.

"What's that mess by the door?" said Rama. She went to see what it was. There were dirty paw prints going out into the hall. "At last, a clue!" shouted Rama. She ran into the backyard and peeked into the doghouse. There was Sofie, and there was the missing blue shoe. The mystery was solved!

Rama took the shoe out of the doghouse. It was dirty and the heel had been chewed on. Rama ran back into the house yelling, "Mom! Look what Sofie did to my shoe!"

Questions about
The Mystery of the Missing Blue Shoe

1. Why was Rama happy at the beginning of the story?

_____

2. What happened to make her unhappy?

_____

3. Where did she look for the blue shoe?

_____

4. Why did Rama know that:

   her little sister didn't take the shoe?

   _____

   her brother didn't take the shoe?

   _____

5. What clue led Rama to her shoe?

_____

6. How did she feel when she looked at the shoe?

_____

7. What do you think Rama will do with the shoe?

_____

Think about It

Rama found a boot, three socks, and a dog bone under her bed. On the back of this page, tell what you would find if you looked under your bed.

Name _____

What Does It Mean?

Match each word to its meaning.

1. wear   gone or lost

2. missing   a question; something that needs to be solved

3. mystery   to have on as clothing

4. problem   untidy; dirty

5. messy   to find the answer to a problem

6. clue   something that can't be explained; a puzzle

7. solve   a hint that helps solve a mystery

Find a word in the story that:

1. means **the end of a bed**   _____

2. rhymes with **new**   _____

3. is the opposite of **left**   _____

Two, To, Too

Fill in the missing words.

1. Rama's little sister is _____ years old.

2. Rama has a brother, _____.

3. Sofie took the shoe _____ her doghouse.

Name _____

Spelling oo

Circle the letters that say **oo**.

shoes	blue	few
school	boot	two
new	who	clue

Fill in the missing letter or letters.

sh_____es

b_____t

tw_____

They Go Together

1. **glove** is to **hand** as **shoe** is to _____

2. **on** is to **off** as **in** is to _____

3. **milk** is to **drink** as **cookie** is to _____

4. **sky** is to **blue** as **grass** is to _____

5. **bird** is to **fly** as **fish** is to _____

6. **round** is to **shape** as **blue** is to _____

7. **princess** is to **queen** as **prince** is to _____

8. **bat** is to **cave** as **bee** is to _____

Name _____

What Happened Next?

Read, cut, and paste in order.

1.

2.

3.

4.

5.

6.

✂- -

One of Rama's new blue shoes was missing.

Her brother did not take the shoe.

Rama found the missing shoe in Sofie's doghouse.

Rama got new blue shoes with silver buckles.

Her little sister did not take the shoe.

Rama found a clue. It was a dirty paw print.

Name _____

On My Feet

Make a list of things you can wear on your feet.

_____   _____

_____   _____

_____   _____

_____   _____

_____   _____

Draw:

Rama's new shoes	shoes you would like to buy

The Fox and the Crow

Long ago, there was a very vain crow. "I'm sure you have never seen feathers more handsome than mine," he bragged to everyone he met. "I'm sure you have never heard a voice more musical than mine."

One day in the forest, the crow found a hunk of cheese someone had dropped. The crow swooped down and picked up the cheese with his strong beak. He flew up to the top of the fence and started to eat the cheese.

Just then a hungry fox strolled by. When he saw the cheese in the crow's beak, the fox thought, "That looks like a good snack for me."

The fox knew he would have to trick the crow to get the cheese. The fox sat thinking. Soon he had an idea.

"I hope you don't mind if I sit here and look at you," said the fox to the crow. "I've never seen such shiny black feathers." The crow liked the compliment, but he still sat quietly, holding on to the cheese.

"I have heard that your song is sweeter than any other bird's. Is that true?" the fox asked the crow.

The vain crow was eager to show the fox how beautiful he sounded. He opened his beak and started to caw. Down fell the cheese to the ground. The clever fox grabbed the cheese and gobbled it up.

As he hurried down the path, the fox called back, "You may be beautiful, but you are not very smart. You should never trust a flatterer."

Name _____

Questions about *The Fox and the Crow*

1. How did the crow show that he was vain?

_____

2. What did the crow do after he found the cheese?

_____

3. What did the fox think when he strolled by the crow?

_____

4. How did the fox get the cheese away from the crow?

_____

5. Write two words that describe:

       the crow   the fox

    _____   _____

    _____   _____

6. What lesson did the crow learn?

_____

Think about It

Why do you think the crow was always bragging about himself?

_____

_____

_____

Name _____

What Does It Mean?

Match each word to its meaning.

1. vain

2. musical

3. hunk

4. strolled

5. compliment

6. eager

7. clever

8. brag

9. flatterer

a big lump or piece of something

in a hurry to begin

sounding beautiful or pleasing to the ear

very smart or skillful

having too much pride in your looks or abilities

walked slowly

something nice said about someone

someone who gives untrue praise or praises too much

to speak too highly of yourself

Who Am I?

Who does each riddle tell about? Draw the answer.

I used flattery to get what I wanted. Who am I?	I was so vain about my looks and voice that I was tricked out of my snack. Who am I?

         More Read and Understand • Grade 3 • EMC 747

Name _____

Sounds of Short Vowels

Write each word in the box that shows the correct short vowel sound.

aunt   hunk   pick   of   hymn
best   held   fox   fell   met
have   dance   trick   bought   bottle
drop   with   such   come   ran

a	e	i	o	u

Sounds of *th*

Make an **X** on the words with the sound **th** as in **the**.
Make a circle around the words with the sound **th** as in **thin**.

the   these   three

they   thorns   that

thousand   thing   weather

thick   there   with

Name _____

Add a Suffix

Write each base word with a suffix.

1. Just add **ed** and **ing**.

pick   _____   _____

start   _____   _____

2. Double the last letter and add the endings **ed** and **ing**.

drop   _____   _____

grab   _____   _____

3. Change **y** to **i** and add the ending **ed**.

hurry   _____

study   _____

4. Just add the ending **ing**.

hurry   _____

study   _____

Fill in the missing words.

1. The vain crow _____ the cheese when he

_____ to caw.

2. The fox _____ the cheese and

_____ down the path.

Name _____

Verbs

Verbs are action words. Circle the verbs in this list. Then find the words you circled in the word search.

walk	(stroll)	pick	flew
heard	thought	think	when
fence	cheese	ask	grab
open	bright	hungry	fox
called	swoop	sit	brag

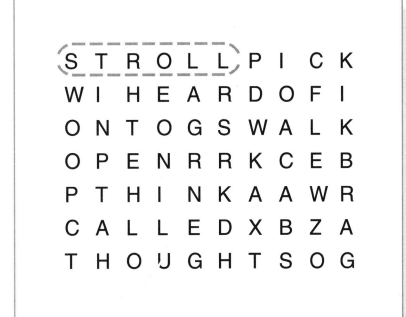

```
S T R O L L P I C K
W I H E A R D O F I
O N T O G S W A L K
O P E N R R K C E B
P T H I N K A A W R
C A L L E D X B Z A
T H O U G H T S O G
```

Circle the verbs in these sentences.

1. A crow picked up a hunk of cheese and flew over to the fence.

2. A hungry fox strolled by and saw the crow.

3. When the crow opened his beak, the cheese fell to the ground.

4. The fox thought of a way to make the crow drop the cheese.

5. The fox grabbed the cheese and gobbled it up.

...ie' ...a ati...n Diary

June 10

Dear Diary,

Tonight my dad came home, sat down, and kicked off his shoes. "I need a vacation," he announced.

The rest of us think that's a great idea. Mom is going to call Aunt Myrtle and see if we can visit her. Aunt Myrtle lives at the beach.

June 15

Dear Diary,

This has been a terrible day! We got up early and packed the car. Then we waited and waited. The pet sitter was very late. She was very sorry. Her alarm clock was broken and she overslept.

We all climbed into the car. I was the first one in, so I got to sit by a window. Then my brothers started fighting. They both wanted the other window. Nobody in our family likes to sit in the middle. Dad told them to be quiet and let my little brother, Tony, have the window first. It wasn't long before he started asking, "Are we there yet?" That drives my dad nuts.

To make it a really great day, we heard "Lub-dub, lub-dub." Dad got out and started yelling. We had a flat tire! Everyone got out of the car. We took everything out of the trunk so Dad could get the spare tire and jack. After he had put on the spare, Dad drove to a gas station to get the tire fixed. We had snacks from a vending machine while we waited.

As soon as we got back on the road, Tony said, "I've got to go to the bathroom."

Dad pointed out that we had just been at a gas station. "Why didn't you go while we were there?" he asked. So we stopped again.

The car finally pulled in at Aunt Myrtle's at 10:00 p.m. We were all asleep in the backseat. Mom carried Tony in, and the rest of us carried in the luggage.

June 16

Dear Diary,

That awful trip yesterday was worth it! It's beautiful here. The beach is just outside Aunt Myrtle's door. David, my big brother, is so excited. He is going surfing with our cousins. Dad already left to go deep-sea fishing. The rest of us are going to the beach. Tony has his bucket and shovel. Mom has a book to read. I'm taking my camera. I can hardly wait to take pictures of the waves and rocks.

Still June 16

Dear Diary,

We just got back from the beach. We're all wet and covered with sand, but it was great! Tony built a huge sand castle. He found some little hermit crabs in a shallow tide pool. Tony cried a little when Aunt Myrtle told him the hermit crabs had to stay at the beach. He had already given them names!

I took two rolls of pictures. I can't wait to get the film developed. Tomorrow Aunt Myrtle is taking us out on her sailboat. Maybe we'll see a whale or some porpoises.

June 20

Dear Diary,

We've been so busy I haven't had time to write. We're all a little sad. We have to go home tomorrow. This has been the very best vacation of all time! I can't wait to come back again.

Name _____

Questions about
Rosie's Vacation Diary

1. What was Dad's great idea?

   _____

2. Where did the family go on vacation?

   _____

3. Give two reasons the family was late getting to Aunt Myrtle's house.

   _____   _____

4. What did each person do on June 16?

   Dad _____   Rosie _____

   Mom _____   Tony _____

   David _____

5. Why would someone keep a diary?

   _____

Problem	Solution
Both boys wanted to sit in the backseat by the window.	_____ _____
_____ _____	Dad got out the spare tire and the jack to put it on. Then he drove to a gas station.

Name _____

What Does It Mean?

Match each word to its meaning.

1. diary

2. beach

3. alarm

4. middle

5. vending machine

6. luggage

7. shallow

8. sitter

a bell or other device to warn or waken people

halfway between; in the center

a book in which you write down what happens each day

suitcases or other bags carried by a traveler

a shore area of sand or pebbles along the ocean

not deep

a person who watches someone's children, pets, or belongings

a machine from which you get candy, stamps, or other objects when money is dropped in

Name the pictures.

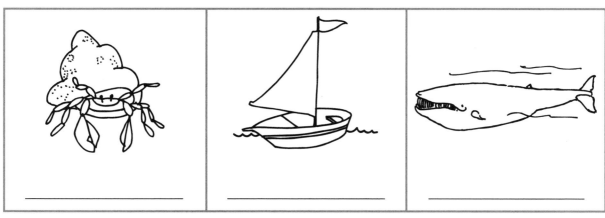

_____ _____ _____

Name _____

Spell Long *i*

The sound of long **i** is spelled many ways.

      i–e in m**i**n**e**   **igh** in fl**igh**t   **i** in **i**tem   **y** in sh**y**

Fill in the missing letters in these words and sentences.

    dr____v____   cr____   s____t   wr____t____

    n____t   l____   sk____   p____

1. Rosie saw a bird fl____ing overhead.

2. Her brothers were f____ting in the backseat.

3. Dad had a great ____dea.

4. "Lub–dub," went the flat t____r____.

Homophones

Homophones are words that sound the same. They are spelled differently and have different meanings.

Find the homophones for these words in the story.

1. grate	_____	5. see	_____
2. too	_____	6. reed	_____
3. wee	_____	7. sum	_____
4. knead	_____	8. weight	_____

On the back of this page, write a sentence using each of these words:

            weight   wait

How Did They Feel?

Use these words to describe how the characters in the story felt.

happy	angry	upset	thankful
calm	excited	impatient	relieved

1. How did Rosie feel when Aunt Myrtle said she could go out on the sailboat?

   Rosie felt _____.

2. How did Dad feel when he saw the flat tire?

   Dad felt _____.

3. How did Mom feel when she read a book at the beach?

   Mom felt _____.

4. How did the family feel as they waited for the pet sitter?

   They felt _____.

5. How did Aunt Myrtle feel when the family finally arrived?

   Aunt Myrtle felt _____.

What Happened Next?

Number the events in order.

_____ The family packed the car to go to the beach.

_____ The family had fun at the beach.

_____ Dad said that he needed a vacation.

_____ They finally arrived at Aunt Myrtle's at 10:00 p.m.

_____ The pet sitter overslept, making them late.

The Stubborn Little Hen

Butter was a small, round hen. She was as yellow as a cube of butter. That's how she got her name. Butter lived in a coop in the barnyard. There were a dozen other hens and a handsome red rooster. Almost every day, Butter laid a little brown egg.

A few weeks ago, Butter began to sit on the eggs in her nest. Hens do this when they are ready to hatch baby chicks. The farmer had all the chickens he wanted, so he took the eggs out of Butter's nest.

When the farmer took her eggs, Butter would sit on the eggs of other hens. Day after day, Butter sat on eggs. She sat on big eggs and small eggs. She sat on brown eggs and white eggs. Butter didn't care. She was ready to be a mother.

Then one day, Butter disappeared. The farmer looked around but couldn't find her. He felt sad. "A hawk or a fox must have caught her," he thought.

Four weeks later, the farmer saw a wonderful sight. Here came Butter, followed by three tiny, fluffy chicks. "You clever little lady," chuckled the farmer. "I see you found a way to keep your eggs after all."

The farmer gently picked up Butter and her babies. He carried them into the coop. "I guess we can make room for three more little hens," he said. "I think I'll call you Peanut, Little Bit, and Fluffy."

Name _____

Questions about
The Stubborn Little Hen

1. What kind of animal is Butter? Describe her.

_____

2. Why did Butter sit on the eggs?

_____

3. Why did the farmer keep taking the eggs away from Butter?

_____

4. What did the farmer think when Butter disappeared?

_____

5. What did Butter do while she was gone?

_____

6. Why do you think the farmer decided to make room for the new little chicks?

_____

Think about It

The hens laid eggs almost every day. What could the farmer do with all those eggs?

_____

_____

_____

Name _____

What Does It Mean?

Match each word to its meaning.

1. clever   to go out of sight; vanish

2. disappear   to laugh

3. dozen   smart

4. hatch   won't give up

5. chuckle   a pen for chickens

6. gently   12 of anything

7. stubborn   to break out of an egg

8. coop   kindly; carefully

Draw pictures for these phrases.

small yellow hen	handsome red rooster	three tiny, fluffy chicks

Name _____

Sounds of ow

Read the words. Write them in the correct boxes.

brown   follow   allow
blow   own   flower
crowd   tow   clown
flown   tower   sown

ow in n**ow**	long **o** in cr**ow**
_____	_____
_____	_____
_____	_____
_____	_____
_____	_____

Categories

Make a ✓ by the word that does not belong. Write a title for each category.

_____	_____	_____
category title	category title	category title
feather	coop	hen
beak	garage	chick
claws	barn	goose
hair	sty	rooster

Name _____

Antonyms

Find a word in the story that is the opposite of each word.

1. large _____   6. stood _____

2. night _____   7. father _____

3. give _____   8. lost _____

4. less _____   9. died _____

5. could _____   10. appeared _____

Adjectives

Adjectives describe things. Circle the words that describe Butter.

yellow	large	stubborn
lazy	round	small
busy	clever	tall

Write one sentence about Butter, using at least three of the words you circled.

_____

_____

_____

Name _____

What Happened Next?

Read, cut, and paste the sentences in order.

1. [   ]

2. [   ]

3. [   ]

4. [   ]

5. [   ]

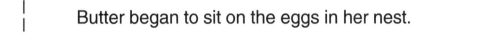

Butter began to sit on the eggs in her nest.

Butter came back, followed by three tiny, fluffy chicks.

The farmer took the eggs out of Butter's nest.

Butter laid a little brown egg almost every day.

The farmer could not find Butter. She had disappeared.

Hand-Me-Downs

A large box arrived for Ginny. It was from her cousin Peggy. When Ginny opened the box, it was packed full of used clothes. Peggy was a year older and a little bit bigger than Ginny. She was always sending Ginny the clothes she had outgrown.

"Mother, do I have to wear Peggy's old clothes again this year?" complained Ginny.

"Don't you like the nice things Peggy sends?" asked Mother. She began to pull things out of the box. "How about these denim overalls? I thought you liked them when Peggy wore them to your birthday party. And here's that cute vest you admired."

"They're okay," Ginny admitted. "I'd just like to have something new, too."

"I understand," said Mother. "How would you like to go to Giant Mart on Saturday? We can get you a new shirt to go with the overalls and maybe a skirt to wear with the vest. Would that make you feel better?"

Ginny jumped up and gave her mother a huge hug. "Yes, that will make me feel much better."

"I have another hand-me-down to show you," said Mother. She went to her jewelry box and took out a locket. "This locket was handed down from your great-grandmother to your grandmother. Your grandmother handed it down to me. Someday I will hand it down to you. So you see how precious a hand-me-down can be." Mother opened the locket to show Ginny the pictures of her great-grandmother and her great-grandfather.

Name _____

Questions about *Hand-Me-Downs*

1. What was in the box that came for Ginny?

_____

2. Name something to wear that came in the box.

_____

3. Why did Ginny complain to her mother?

_____

4. How did Mother get the locket she showed Ginny?

_____

5. Why did Peggy send her hand-me-downs to Ginny?

_____

Think about It

What happens to the clothes you outgrow?

_____

_____

_____

_____

Name _____

What Does It Mean?

Write the words by their meanings.

cousin   hand-me-downs
denim   huge
great-grandmother   precious

1. worth a lot   _____

2. your grandmother's mother   _____

3. a child of your aunt or uncle   _____

4. a heavy cotton cloth   _____

5. used items given to another person _____

6. very large   _____

Name the pictures.

_____   _____   _____

Name _____

Sounds of g

Write the sound the letter **g** makes in these words. Write **g** or **j** on the lines.

1. Ginny _____   7. edge _____

2. huge _____   8. hug _____

3. Peggy _____   9. garden _____

4. girl _____   10. gem _____

5. giant _____   11. age _____

6. get _____   12. gave _____

Rhyming Words

Find words in the story that rhyme with these words.

1. bug _____   6. deer _____

2. pocket _____   7. few _____

3. nest _____   8. pear _____

4. dozen _____   9. brother _____

5. hose _____   10. bee _____

Name _____

Word Webs

Write the correct word in each box. You will not use all of
the words.

cousin	vest	locket	son
uncle	ring	mother	necklace
overalls	shirt	bracelet	sweater
coat	pin	aunt	
watch	niece	pants	

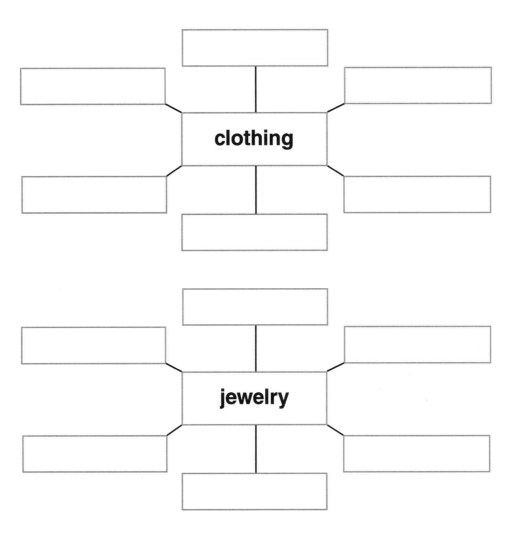

clothing

jewelry

Look at the words you did not use. They belong together.

Give them a name. _____

Name _____

Thank You, Peggy

Pretend you are Ginny. Write a thank-you letter for the box of clothes.

Dear Peggy,

Your cousin,
Ginny

The Princess and the Pea

Once upon a time there was a prince who was looking for a bride. "You must marry a real princess," said his father, the king.

The unmarried women of the kingdom were happy to hear that the prince was looking for a bride. Many young women came to the palace hoping to become his bride.

"How can I tell who is a real princess and who is not?" the prince wondered. He went to his mother, the queen, for advice.

"We must think of a test, my son," said the queen. She thought and thought. Finally, the queen had an idea. "A real princess is very delicate. She is unable to sleep if there is even a tiny lump in her bed. I have thought of a way we can find a real princess for you to marry."

Each young woman who came to the castle was asked to spend the night. After dinner, she was led to the bedchamber. The bed was piled high with soft mattresses. In the morning, the queen would ask the same question, "How did you sleep last night?"

Each morning she received the same answer. "I slept very well. It is a comfortable bed." The prince began to think he would never find a bride.

One stormy night, there was a knock at the door. When the door was opened, in walked a bedraggled girl. She was soaking wet from head to toe.

"My coach broke down in the storm. May I please have a bed for the night?" she said.

The queen led the girl to the bedchamber and gave her a dry nightgown. "Sweet dreams," said the queen as she shut the door.

The next morning the queen asked, "How did you sleep last night?"

The girl answered, "I could not sleep at all. That is the most uncomfortable bed I have ever slept in."

The queen began to smile. She reached under the pile of mattresses and pulled out a small dried pea.

"This is why you could not sleep," explained the queen. "Only a real princess is so delicate. At last we have found a bride for the prince."

Questions about
The Princess and the Pea

1. What did the king tell the prince when he started looking for a bride?

   _____

2. Who did the prince go to for advice?

   _____

3. Describe the test the queen used to find a real princess.

   _____

4. Why did the queen think her test would work?

   _____

5. Which of the young women who took the queen's test turned out to be a real princess?

   _____

6. Do you think this test really proved who was a real princess? Why?

   _____

Think about It

The queen thought of a test to find a real princess for her son to marry. Use your imagination and plan another test to find a real princess. Write your plan here.

_____

_____

_____

Name _____

What Does It Mean?

Match each word to its meaning.

1. bride   a room for sleeping

2. kingdom   a woman just married or to be married

3. advice   wet and untidy

4. delicate   an idea about what should be done

5. lump   easily hurt and needing special care

6. bedchamber   a small, solid hunk

7. mattress   a country governed by a king or a queen

8. bedraggled   a thick pad used for a bed

What does **sweet dreams** mean? _____

What does **soaking wet** mean? _____

The Prefix *Un*

The prefix **un** means **not**. Add **un** to these words. Use the new words
in sentences.

____comfortable   ____happy   ____married   ____able

1. _____

2. _____

3. _____

4. _____

Name _____

Long Vowel Sounds

Write the long vowel sound you hear in each word.

1. coach _____   6. dream _____   11. claim _____

2. night _____   7. pile _____   12. sleep _____

3. pea _____   8. unit _____   13. cute _____

4. so _____   9. frame _____   14. break _____

5. bride _____   10. cube _____   15. soaked _____

More Than One

Words that name more than one of something are called **plurals**.
Add **s** or **es** to make the plural of most words.
Change **y** at the end to **i** and add **es** to make the plural of some words.

1. dream _____   5. princess _____

2. mattress _____   6. coach _____

3. pea _____   7. story _____

4. berry _____   8. kingdom _____

A few words have special plurals. Write the words that mean more than one.

1. woman _____   3. goose _____

2. child _____   4. man _____

Name _____

Problems and Solutions

Find the problems and the solutions. Write them on the lines.

1. Sherry wanted a new bike like the one her friend Tanya got for her birthday. Her parents told her that there was nothing wrong with her old bike. Sherry finally talked her parents into letting her get the new bike. There was just one problem. She had to earn half the money it would cost.

   Sherry thought about what she could do. Then she went from door to door in her neighborhood asking people she knew for jobs. She explained that she knew how to baby-sit, mow lawns, and run errands. Soon she was busily working every weekend.

   Problem   Solution

   _____   _____

   _____   _____

   _____   _____

2. Hi! I'm Harry. The muscles in my arms and legs are weak. I can't use my legs at all, and I'm not too great with my hands. If I drop something, it stays dropped until someone picks it up for me. I have an electric wheelchair to help me move around. I have a golden retriever that has been trained to pick up things I drop. I'm happy to have such a good four-legged friend.

   Problem   Solution

   _____   _____

   _____   _____

   _____   _____

What Happened Next?

Number the sentences in order.

_____ The queen had an idea. She piled a bed high with soft mattresses and put a dried pea under them.

_____ The prince went to his mother to ask how to find a real princess.

_____ The next morning the girl said, "I could not sleep at all in that uncomfortable bed."

_____ Many young women came claiming to be real princesses, but they all failed the test.

_____ One stormy night, a bedraggled girl appeared at the door. The queen led her to the bedchamber and wished her sweet dreams.

_____ Once long ago, there was a prince who was looking for a bride. "You must marry a real princess," said his father, the king.

_____ The queen was very happy. "At last we have found a bride for the prince."

The Queen

How do you think the queen felt when:

1. the prince asked for her advice? _____

2. she had an idea for a test to find a real princess? _____

3. the young women kept telling her how well they had slept? _____

4. she knew the bedraggled girl was a real princess? _____

Computer Mouse

Thomas is a little brown mouse. He lives in the wall of Peter's bedroom. Peter doesn't know he has a houseguest. Thomas only comes out when Peter is gone.

One day after Peter left, Thomas came out of his hole in the wall. He saw something new on Peter's desk. Thomas jumped up onto the desk. He walked around the strange box he found there. Suddenly there was a bright light on one side of the box. Somehow Thomas had bumped a switch and turned on Peter's computer. Thomas hopped off the desk and ran home.

An hour later, Peter returned. "Oh, no! I forgot to turn off my computer," groaned Peter. Since the computer was on, Peter began to work on a report for school. He didn't see the tiny face peeking around the edge of the computer. Without a sound, Thomas had slipped up to watch Peter.

"Peter," called Dad, "can you come here for a minute?" Peter went to see what his father wanted.

Thomas jumped up onto the computer mouse. The screen changed. Then he hopped onto the keyboard. As he hopped around, letters started to appear on the screen. When he heard Peter coming back, Thomas hid behind the computer.

"How did that happen? That isn't what I wrote. What is going on here?" said Peter with a frown. Thomas didn't make a sound. He didn't move.

Peter ran to get his dad. "Something weird is going on, Dad," he said.

Dad and Peter stood quietly by the bedroom door. "Sh, Peter. Don't make a sound," whispered Dad.

Thomas listened for a few minutes. It was very quiet in the bedroom. Thomas moved out from his hiding place. He hopped back up onto the keyboard. "Look!" shouted Peter. When Thomas heard that loud sound, off he shot like a rocket.

"It looks like you have a new computer mouse," said Dad, laughing.

Questions about *Computer Mouse*

1. Who was:

    Peter?   _____

    Thomas?   _____

2. Where did Thomas live?

    _____

3. How did Thomas:

    turn on the computer?   _____

    type letters?   _____

4. How did Peter and Dad find out about Thomas?

    _____

5. Why did Dad call Thomas a computer mouse?

    _____

6. What do you think will happen to Thomas?

Think about It

What would you do if you found a mouse in your bedroom?

_____

_____

_____

Name _____

What Does It Mean?

Match each word to its meaning.

1. houseguest   to see; to observe

2. switch   a device for turning a machine off and on

3. watch   to speak softly

4. weird   a visitor to your home

5. whisper   strange; odd

What are the two meanings for **mouse** in the story?

_____

What does **off he shot like a rocket** mean?

_____

Use these words in sentences to show you know what they mean.

      switch   weird   houseguest

1. _____

2. _____

3. _____

Name _____

Spelling **ou**

The sound **ou** can be spelled **ou** (s**ou**nd) and **ow** (t**ow**n).

m____se   br____n   h____r

fr____n   n____   f____nd

____t   h____se   h____

sh____t   d____n   r____nd

Silent Letters

Read the words. Cross out the letters that don't make a sound.

Thomas   listen   know
write   talk   sign

Use the past-tense form of three words above to fill in the blanks.

1. Peter _____ the report on his computer.

2. Peter _____ something weird was going on.

3. Thomas _____ carefully to see if anyone was in the bedroom.

4. Peter _____ to his dad about the strange things happening in his room.

Name _____

Peter and Thomas

1. Write your name on the computer screen.

2. Make an **X** on the keyboard.

3. Color the desk dark brown and the computer light brown.

4. Draw:
        a. a hole in the wall where Thomas lives
        b. Thomas sitting on the computer mouse
        c. Dad and Peter peeking around the door

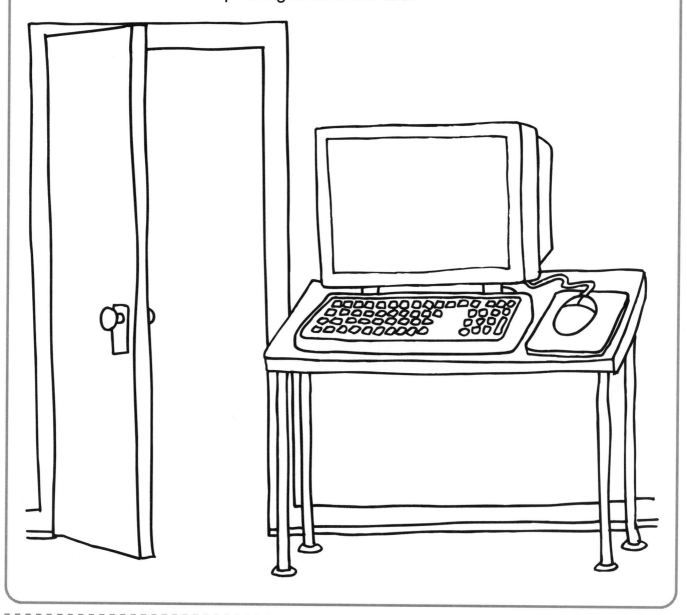

Name _____

What Happened Next?

Pretend you are Peter in *Computer Mouse*. Write a letter to a friend. Explain what happened in the story.

Dear

Your friend,
Peter

Paddy and the Giant Potato

"I'd like a wee bit of potato for my supper," thought Paddy the leprechaun. He knew just where there was a field of potatoes ready to dig up. "I'll just drop by Sean O'Toole's farm. I'm sure he won't mind if I borrow a potato or two," said Paddy.

When Paddy reached the farm, he quickly dug up a potato. He hurried back home to cook it. "There's nothing like a boiled potato," he said as he licked the last few bits of potato off his fingers.

The next day about suppertime, Paddy began thinking about that delicious potato. "I'm sure Sean won't mind if I borrow another potato. After all, he has a whole field of them." Off he went to Sean's farm.

Paddy turned over the soil and spied the tip of a potato. "That looks like a good one," he thought. He reached down and pulled on the end of the potato. Nothing happened. He pulled harder. The potato still didn't move. Paddy dug in his heels and pulled as hard as he could. The potato wiggled, but it was still stuck in the ground.

It looked like a new plan was necessary. Paddy thought and thought. "I'll get someone to help pull the potato loose," he said.

First, he called on his friend Michael. Paddy pulled the potato and Michael pulled Paddy. Still the potato did not move.

Then Paddy called on his friend Finn. Paddy took hold of the potato, Michael held on to Paddy, and Finn held on to Michael. "All right, lads. At the count of three, pull with all your might," said Paddy.

"One. Two. Three!" They all pulled as hard as they could. Up, up, up came the potato. It was the biggest potato any of the leprechauns had ever seen. The leprechauns jumped up and down and yelled, "Hip, hip, hooray!"

Sean O'Toole came out to see what all the noise was about. He saw the leprechauns taking his potato. "You scoundrels! Drop that potato." He ran across the field after the leprechauns.

"Come on, lads. Let's get out of here!" shouted Paddy. With the help of a little leprechaun magic, the friends escaped with the giant potato.

"Will you stay and have a bit of supper with me?" asked Paddy. "I think there's enough potato for all of us."

Name _____

Questions about
Paddy and the Giant Potato

1. What kind of creatures are Paddy, Michael, and Finn?

   _____

2. Where was Paddy getting his potatoes?

   _____

3. What did Paddy really mean when he said he was going to "borrow" a potato from Sean O'Toole?

   _____

4. Why did Paddy have to call on his friends for help?

   _____

5. Was Sean O'Toole upset when he saw the leprechauns taking potatoes from his field? Explain your answer.

   _____

   _____

6. How did the leprechauns escape?

   _____

Think about It

Imagine you are Paddy the leprechaun. Think of a way to get the giant potato out of the ground without any help.

_____

_____

_____

Name _____

What Does It Mean?

Find a word in the story that means:

1. a dwarflike creature in Irish folktales   _____

2. open land used for crops or a pasture   _____

3. to get something from another person
   with the understanding that it will be returned   _____

4. good tasting   _____

5. caught sight of   _____

6. rascals; persons of bad character   _____

7. got away from   _____

Use these words in sentences to show you know what they mean.

enough   magic   tasty

1. _____

_____

2. _____

_____

3. _____

_____

Name _____

More Than One

Fill in the missing words in this paragraph by writing the plural form of each word.

The _____ were digging up _____ in
         child   potato

Uncle Kevin's garden. They heard _____ coming from the
                                         noise

_____ by the fence. They ran over to see what was making the
       bush

noise. A tiny face was peeking out from between the _____.
                                                leaf

It was a bunny. The children looked under the bush and saw three more

_____.
   bunny

Contractions

Write the words that make these contractions.

I'll _____   won't _____

we'll _____   shouldn't _____

they'll _____   haven't _____

What does the 'll replace? _____   What does the n't replace? _____

he's _____   we've _____

there's _____   they've _____

it's _____   I've _____

What does the 's replace? _____   What does the 've replace? _____

Name _____

Potatoes

Ask 10 classmates to name their favorite way to eat potatoes.
Complete this list.

person asked	favorite way to eat potatoes
1. _____	1. _____
2. _____	2. _____
3. _____	3. _____
4. _____	4. _____
5. _____	5. _____
6. _____	6. _____
7. _____	7. _____
8. _____	8. _____
9. _____	9. _____
10. _____	10. _____

Write about the way you like potatoes to be cooked. Give at least two
reasons why you like them that way.

_____

_____

_____

_____

Name _____

Catch a Leprechaun

An old folktale says that if you catch a leprechaun, he must give you his pot of gold. Explain how you would catch a leprechaun. Then draw a leprechaun sitting on top of his pot of gold.

     60   More Read and Understand • Grade 3 • EMC 747

Little Bat

Small and furry,
little bat,
fly through the sky at night.

Listen, listen,
little bat,
as echoes guide your flight.

Now swoop and dive,
little bat,
catch insects as you fly.

Hurry, hurry,
little bat,
back to your cave nearby.

All snug and warm,
little bat,
toes hold the ceiling tight.

Sleepy, sleepy,
little bat,
wrapped in your wings 'til night.

Name _____

Questions about *Little Bat*

1. At what time of day did the bat fly?

   _____

2. How does the bat find its way around?

   _____

3. What words in the poem tell how the bat moves?

   _____   _____   _____

4. What does the bat eat?

   _____

5. Where does the bat sleep?

   _____

6. How are bats helpful to humans?

   _____

   _____

Think about It

Make a list of things that fly. Circle the "flyers" that are alive. Make an **X** on "flyers" that are not alive.

   _____   _____   _____

   _____   _____   _____

   _____   _____   _____

What Does It Mean?

Write a word in the poem that means:

1. repeated sounds   _____

2. to come down in a rush   _____

3. comfortable and sheltered   _____

4. a hollow space underground   _____

5. not far away   _____

6. to show the way   _____

7. the top of a room or a cave   _____

Homophones

Homophones are words that sound the same but are not spelled the same. Homophones have different meanings.

Find homophones for these words in the *Little Bat* poem.

1. sealing _____   2. threw _____   3. tows _____

Fill in the missing homophones.

1. Arnold _____ a ball _____ Mrs. Carter's window.

2. Dad is _____ a crack in the _____ with plaster.

3. Carl gets his _____ wet when he _____ his boat in the water.

Name _____

Rhyming Words

Find a word in the poem that rhymes with each of these words.
Write another word that rhymes with each word.

1. night _____ _____

2. nearby _____ _____

Word Families

A word family is made of words that are the same except for the beginning sounds. The words **hay**, **day**, and **stray** are in the same word family.

Use the following clues to help you find members of the two word families.

light		**end**	
1. to do battle	____ight	1. to repair a broken object	____end
2. to correct	____ight	2. not straight, curve	____end
3. opposite of loose	____ight	3. to let someone borrow	____end
4. opposite of day	____ight	4. to cause something to go from one place to another	____end
5. a trip by airplane	____ight	5. to take care of	____end
6. sudden fear	____ight	6. to mix together	____end
7. ability to see	____ight	7. to pay out money	____end

Name _____

Sounds of y at the End

Read the words. Write the sound of the letter **y**.

1. sky ____   6. fly ____

2. furry ____   7. why ____

3. nearby ____   8. only ____

4. busy ____   9. many ____

5. angry ____   10. shy ____

At the end of one-syllable words **y** says _____.

At the end of two-syllable words **y** says _____.

Syllable Count

Write the words in the correct boxes.

furry   echo   little   sleepy   insect
night   guide   warm   swamp   through
listen   wrapped   nearby   cave

one syllable	two syllables
_____	_____
_____	_____
_____	_____
_____	_____
_____	_____
_____	_____

Name _____

Bats

Read the poem *Little Bat* again.
List eight facts about bats that are named in the poem.

1. _____

2. _____

3. _____

4. _____

5. _____

6. _____

7. _____

8. _____

Bats

There are almost 1,000 kinds of bats throughout the world. Some are as small as a jelly bean. Some are as big as a small dog. Bats come in many colors and patterns. This helps bats blend in with their surroundings.

Bats are mammals. They have furry bodies. Female bats have live babies that drink milk from the mother's body.

Bats are the only mammals that can really fly. Bats' wings are made of muscle, bone, and skin. Strong chest muscles help flap the wings. The bones in a bat's wing are a lot like the bones in a human hand. The wing has four long bones and a little thumb that sticks out at the front. The bat uses the thumb to help it move around its roost. Bats use their tails for balance and making turns. They use curved claws on their feet to hold on when they roost. Bats hang upside down and don't fall, even when sleeping.

An insect-eating bat uses its voice and hearing to find food. This is called echolocation. A bat makes squeaks and clicks. The sounds bounce off trees, insects, and other objects. An insect-eating bat's big ears catch the sounds as they return. A bat can tell how far away the object is. It can tell what direction to fly in to get to the object. A bat can even tell how big the object is. It catches insects as it flies through the air. Every night insect-eating bats eat millions of insects that might destroy our crops.

A fruit-eating bat uses its eyes and sense of smell to find food. It may eat fruit, flowers, or nectar. It has smaller ears than an insect-eater. Some fruit-eating bats have noses with strange flaps that catch smells better. Fruit-eating bats spread pollen from plant to plant as they eat. They also carry seeds from one place to another. This helps new plants grow.

Bats eat other things, too. There are bats that eat frogs, rodents, fish, and other small animals. Vampire bats live on blood.

Bats live in groups called colonies. Bat colonies live in dark caves, hollow logs, holes in trees, or in tunnels made by other animals. Some bat colonies live under bridges or in people's barns and attics. Fruit-eating bats often live in trees. One kind of bat even makes a leaf "tent" to use as a home. Some colonies are small. Others have more than one million bats in them.

Name _____

Questions about *Bats*

1. How are bats different from other mammals?

_____

2. Describe a bat's wing.

_____

3. How does a bat use its tail?

_____

4. How does a bat use its curved claws?

_____

5. How does echolocation work?

_____

6. How are bats helpful?

_____

7. What might happen to the earth if all the bats suddenly disappeared?

_____

Think about It

How are bats and birds
the same?

How are bats and
birds different?

_____   _____

_____   _____

_____   _____

Name _____

What Does It Mean?

Match each word to its meaning.

1. surroundings   to spoil or ruin

2. attic   plants grown to be used by people

3. destroy   things or conditions around you

4. crops   in a steady position

5. rodents   a space in a house just below the roof and above the other rooms

6. mammal

7. balanced   a group of animals with large front teeth used for gnawing; rats, mice, squirrels

8. colonies   groups of bats living together

                                  a warm-blooded animal whose babies drink milk from the mother's body

Write the type of bat.

_____-eating bat   _____-eating bat

Name _____

Spell Long e

Circle the letters that say long **e**.

eating	eagle	seeds	leaf
asleep	trees	queen	clean
jelly bean	creep	dream	feet

Fill in the missing letters.

1. I like red jelly b_____ns best.

2. A bald _____gle flew over the tops of the tr_____s.

3. Walter saw a squirrel _____ting s_____ds.

4. Cl_____n your f_____t before you go to bed.

5. The qu_____n fell asl_____p and had a funny dr_____m.

What Says er ?

Circle the letters that say **er** in each of these words.

collar   work   color   earth   her   third   purse

Use the letters you circled to fill in the missing letters below.

1. The doct_____s and n_____ses w_____ked day and night aft_____

   the _____thquake.

2. Moth_____ broke h_____ p_____rl necklace Sat_____day night.

3. From out_____ space astronauts could see the c_____ve of the _____th.

4. The hummingb_____d sucked nect_____ from the flow_____.

Name _____

Bats

Complete the Venn diagram to show how insect-eating bats and fruit-eating bats are alike and different.

insect-eating bat

1. _____

2. _____

3. _____

both

1. _____

2. _____

fruit-eating bat

1. _____

2. _____

3. _____

Name _____

Fact or Opinion?

Check the correct box to show whether each sentence gives a fact or an opinion.

	fact	opinion
1. Bats can fly.	✔	
2. Bats make good pets.		
3. Some bats eat harmful insects.		
4. Bats have furry bodies.		
5. Bats are dirty, harmful animals.		
6. Bats live in colonies.		
7. All bats should be killed.		
8. The bones in a bat's wing are like the bones in a human hand.		

Antonyms

Find a word in the story that is the opposite of each word below.

1. worse _____

2. larger _____

3. drop _____

4. die _____

5. awake _____

6. over _____

7. male _____

8. straight _____

9. lose _____

10. repair _____

Name _____

A Bat's Body

Label the parts of this bat's body.

head	wing	leg	nose
foot	claw	ear	body
thumb	mouth	tail	

The Three Brothers and the Talking Toad

One day an old farmer called his three sons together and said, "A thieving animal is destroying my corn. I will give everything I own to the one of you who stops the animal."

Miguel, the eldest son, set out first. "All I need is a good horse and a gun. I will be back soon," he boasted.

Halfway to the cornfield, Miguel came to a deep well. He stopped to rest and water his horse. Beside the well sat a small toad. The toad said, "If you plan to catch the thief, you need to listen to me."

Miguel was tired and hot. He snapped, "Why should I listen to a toad?" He picked up the small toad, flung it into the well, and continued on his way. He stayed in the cornfield all that afternoon and on into the dark night. But the thieving animal never appeared. Miguel had failed.

The next day, Luis, the second son, set off for the cornfield. When he reached the well, the toad was still there. The toad said, "If you plan to catch the thief, you need to listen to me."

Without a word, Luis picked up the toad and tossed it into the deep well. After a short rest, he rode over to the cornfield. To his surprise, Luis saw a large white bird eating the corn. As the bird took flight, Luis shot at it. Two long tail feathers floated down, but the bird escaped. Luis collected the feathers and trudged home. On the way, he made a plan.

"I have killed the thieving animal," Luis boasted to his father and brothers. "Here are its tail feathers." But his father was not fooled.

"You have only the feathers of the bird. You have not finished the task," said the father. "Now it is your younger brother's turn."

Carlos, the youngest son, set off for the cornfield. When he reached the well, the toad said, "If you plan to catch the thief, you need to listen to me."

Carlos was pleased to see the toad and replied, "Oh, thank you, small toad, for offering your help. If you help me find the thief, I will keep you with me forever."

The toad said, "At the bottom of the well is a magic stone. It will grant you any wish." The toad dove down into the well, brought up the magic stone, and gave it to Carlos.

"I wish for a kind and loving wife and for a way to catch the animal that is stealing my father's corn," said Carlos. He set off to the cornfield with the small toad.

As they reached the cornfield, a large white bird appeared. Carlos took aim, but the toad stopped him. "Please do not shoot me," begged the bird. "I am a girl! An evil witch turned me into a bird when I refused to marry her son."

Carlos was surprised, but he soon realized that his wish was coming true! "Come with me, white bird, and I will take you home to meet my father."

The farmer was shocked to see Carlos returning with a bird and a toad. "I have brought you the thieving animal you asked for, Father. But it is really a girl who was bewitched." They saw the bird change into a lovely young woman right before their eyes.

"You have saved my cornfield," said the farmer. "As I promised, everything I own belongs to you."

Carlos married the young woman, and they lived happily with the old farmer and the small toad. The jealous older brothers ran off and were never seen again.

Name _____

Questions about
The Three Brothers and the Talking Toad

1. What was the farmer's problem?

_____

2. How did the farmer plan to solve his problem?

_____

3. What did the farmer promise his sons?

_____

4. What did the toad tell each brother?

_____

5. Why was the oldest son unable to stop the thief?

_____

6. Why was the second son unable to stop the thief?

_____

7. What happened when the youngest son reached the cornfield?

_____

_____

8. Why were Miguel and Luis jealous of their younger brother?

_____

Think about It

On the back of this page, write about what you think would happen if the older brothers returned. Give a reason for your answer.

Name _____

What Does It Mean?

Match each word to its meaning.

1. thief   to speak too highly about yourself

2. destroy   the time just before dark

3. boast   a person who steals

4. appear   to ruin something or make it useless

5. realize   to come into sight

6. dusk   walked tiredly

7. trudged   to understand clearly

8. task   under a spell

9. bewitched   work to be done

What does **well** mean in this sentence?
        Luis tossed the frog into the **well**.

○ all right

○ a source of water

○ to rise up

What does **change** mean in this sentence?
        They saw the bird **change** into a lovely young woman.

○ to become different

○ money returned when you pay too much

○ to put on different clothes

Name _____

Where Do You Hear Long *e*?

The sound of long **e** can be spelled many ways.

e   **ie**   **ee**   **ea**   final **y**

Circle the letter or letters that spell long **e** in each of these words.

thief	happy	seen	she
three	he	plead	lazy
field	keep	breathe	street
deep	believe	squeal	

Add Endings

Add **er** and **est** to each word.
If the word ends in **y**, change the **y** to **i** and add the ending.

	er	**est**
1. young	_____	_____
2. lazy	_____	_____
3. tiny	_____	_____
4. deep	_____	_____
5. rich	_____	_____
6. happy	_____	_____

Write one sentence using an **er** word and an **est** word.

_____

_____

Name _____

Articles

The articles **a** and **an** come before a noun.
A is used before words starting with a consonant sound.
An is used before words starting with a vowel sound.

_____ old farmer   _____ orange   _____ well

_____ animal   _____ alligator   _____ egg

_____ cornfield   _____ frog   _____ angel

_____ large bird   _____ insect   _____ feather

Compound Words

Circle the compound words in this paragraph. Write the compound words on the lines below. Write each word only one time.

One morning Maryanne looked out her bedroom window and saw blackbirds eating the corn in her cornfield. She ran to the kitchen and grabbed a metal dishpan and a wooden spoon. Out she ran into the cornfield. She banged on the dishpan with the spoon. What a racket she made! Soon all the blackbirds were gone. "I think I'll build a scarecrow this afternoon," she decided. "Maybe that will keep those hungry birds out of my field."

_____   _____

_____   _____

_____   _____

_____   _____

_____

Name _____

Make a ✔ by the words that describe each of the sons.
Some words will have more than one check.

	Miguel	**Luis**	**Carlos**
boastful			
kind			
liar			
unkind			
jealous			
honest			
eager			
successful			

Real or Make-Believe?

The Three Brothers and the Talking Toad contains both real and imaginary events.

List three events in the story that could really happen.

1. _____

2. _____

3. _____

List three events in the story that could not really happen.

1. _____

2. _____

3. _____

Rescue

Walking home from school one day, Rita tripped over her loose shoelace. As she bent over to tie her shoe, Rita heard a sound. It was coming from the alley. She listened for a minute. "That sounds like a dog whimpering," she thought. "I wonder if it's hurt."

Rita walked slowly toward the end of the alley. She saw a pile of broken boxes and garbage. There was a dog lying in the middle of the mess. "Oh, you poor thing! You must be hungry," said Rita. The poor dog was so skinny its ribs stuck out.

Rita tried to get close enough to see if the dog was hurt. Though she wanted to help, she knew better than to try to pick up a strange dog. "I think I'll go get you something to eat," she whispered to the dog.

Rita ran home for food and water. She set the food and dish of water near the dog and then left. She watched from around the corner. She wanted to see what the dog would do. After a few minutes, the hungry dog crept over to the food and water. He ate a little and took a drink of water.

Every day the thoughtful girl brought food to the dog. In a few days she was able to come closer. The dog was looking better. His ribs didn't stick out anymore.

It took a while, but one day her kindness was rewarded. The dog ran up to Rita when she came with food. Carefully Rita reached out and let the dog smell her hand. Then she gently petted his head. When Rita started to leave, she heard footsteps behind her. She peeked over her shoulder and saw the dog following her.

When she reached home, Rita called, "Mother, come and see what I have."

Her mother came to the front door and looked out. "So this is where all the leftovers have been going," she said.

Rita explained how she had found the homeless dog and what she had been doing. "He doesn't have a home, Mother. And he trusts me. I think he would make a good pet. Don't you?" she asked with a hopeful look on her face.

"I guess we can give it a try, but you have to take care of him," said Mother.

They took the little dog to the vet for a checkup. "This is a tough little guy," said the vet. "You've got a good dog here. He'll be fine with good care and lots of love."

When they brought their new pet home, Mother gave the dog a bath. Rita fixed a bed for the dog on the floor by her own bed. The dog took one look at the bed on the floor, hopped up onto Rita's bed, and fell asleep.

Rita was smiling as she climbed into bed. She fell asleep thinking, "I have my very own dog. I wonder what I should name him?"

Name _____

Questions about *Rescue*

1. How did Rita find the dog?

   _____

2. Where was the dog?

   _____

3. How did Rita know the dog was hungry?

   _____

4. What did Rita do to help the dog?

   _____

5. How did she know the dog trusted her?

   _____

6. Why did Rita and her mother take the dog to the vet?

   _____

7. Why do you think the dog decided to sleep on Rita's bed instead of his own?

   _____

8. What do you think would be a good name for the dog? Why?

   _____

Think about It

It could have been dangerous for Rita to go into a dark alley with an unknown animal. On the back of this page, write about what she could have done differently to help the dog.

Name _____

What Does It Mean?

Match each word to its meaning.

1. alley   very thin

2. whimper   food left after a meal

3. skinny   a narrow street in the middle of a city block

4. crept   to whine; a complaining cry

5. kindness   a short name for a doctor who treats animals

6. leftovers   gentleness; helpfulness

7. vet   moved slowly with body close to the ground

Add an Ending

ful means full of
ly means in what manner
less means without

Add the correct endings.

1. in a slow manner   slow_____   5. full of thought   thought_____

2. full of hope   hope_____   6. without harm   harm_____

3. done with care   care_____   7. in a sad way   sad_____

4. without a home   home_____   8. done without care care_____

Name _____

Sounds of *ough*

The phonogram **ough** has many sounds. Write **ough** on the lines.
Read the words and write sentences using each word.

th_____   f_____t   t_____

1. _____

   _____

2. _____

   _____

3. _____

   _____

What Do You Hear?

The letters **gh** can be pronounced like the letter **f** or they can be silent.
Mark what you hear in the following words.

1. tough	(f)	silent	6. laugh	f	silent
2. bought	f	silent	7. enough	f	silent
3. taught	f	silent	8. brought	f	silent
4. rough	f	silent	9. cough	f	silent
5. though	f	silent	10. fought	f	silent

Name _____

Cause and Effect

A **cause** is an event that makes something else happen.
The thing that happens is the **effect**.
Fill in the missing cause and effect below.

Cause	Effect
_____ _____	Rita walked down the alley to see what was making the sound.
Rita brought food to the homeless dog every day.	_____ _____

Dogs

Circle the dogs in the list. Then find the names you circled in the word search.

Angelfish   Dalmatian
Beagle   Greyhound
Bulldog   Hamster
Chihuahua   Husky
Collie   Parakeet
Pekinese   Shepherd
Persian   Siamese
Poodle   Spaniel
Pug   Terrier
Retriever

```
C H I H U A H U A B S M
O U B E A G L E T O H R
L S U P E K I N E S E E
L K L B U L T D O G P T
I Y L D O G C A T R H R
E D D T E R R I E R E I
P O O D L E W D O G R E
X G G S P A N I E L D V
G R E Y H O U N D A L E
D A L M A T I A N T Y R
```

How many times can you find **dog** in the word search? _____

Five Little Chickens

Said the first little chicken
with a strange little squirm,
"I wish I could find
a fat little worm."

Said the second little chicken
with an odd little shrug,
"I wish I could find
a fat little slug."

Said the third little chicken
with a sharp little squeal,
"I wish I could find
some nice yellow meal."

Said the fourth little chicken
with a sigh of grief,
"I wish I could find
a little green leaf."

Said the fifth little chicken,
with a faint little moan,
"I wish I could find
a wee gravel stone."

"Now, see here," said the mother
from the green garden patch,
"If you want your breakfast,
just come here and scratch."

Anonymous

Name _____

Questions about *Five Little Chickens*

1. What did each little chicken want to eat?

   first chicken   _____

   second chicken   _____

   third chicken   _____

   fourth chicken   _____

   fifth chicken   _____

2. Which item does a chicken want that is not food?

   _____

3. What advice did the mother give the little chickens?

   _____

4. During what time of day did the poem take place? How do you know?

   _____

5. What do you think the chickens will scratch up in the garden patch?

   _____

Think about It

Mother told her chickens to get their own breakfast. What would your mother tell you to do for yourself?

   _____

   _____

What Does It Mean?

Read *Five Little Chickens* again. Find the word or words that mean:

1. strange   _____

2. a place to raise plants   _____

3. a little pebble   _____

4. ground up grain   _____

5. a groan   _____

6. not very loud   _____

7. a soft sound of sadness   _____

8. to use claws   _____

Adjectives

Write the words used in the poem to describe these words.

1. _____ _____ squirm

2. _____ _____ squeal

3. _____ _____ moan

4. _____ _____ shrug

5. _____ _____ worm

6. _____ _____ leaf

7. _____ _____ meal

Name _____

What Sound Do You Hear?

These letters make the same sound.

chain   bea**ch**   pa**tch**

Fill in the missing letters.

1. The ____ickens began to scra____ around in the garden pa____.

2. Can you rea____ the pea____ on that tree bran____?

3. Grandfather's pocket wa____ has a long ____ain.

4. We sat on a ben____ and wa____ed the waves move in and out

   along the bea____.

Rhyming Words

Find the words in the poem that rhyme with:

squirm   _____   meal   _____

shrug   _____   grief   _____

patch   _____   stone   _____

Use the words you wrote to fill in the blanks in these sentences.

1. The chicken ran after a long brown _____.

2. She started to _____ when a spider landed on her head.

3. A fat _____ was crawling across a green _____
   on the rosebush.

4. The toothache made Mario _____ in pain.

Name _____

Who Said It?

"I wish I could find a slug," said _____.

"I wish I could find a gravel stone," said _____.

"Just come here and scratch," said _____.

"I wish I could find a worm," said _____.

"I wish I could find a green leaf," said _____.

"Now, see here," said _____.

"I wish I could find some yellow meal," said _____.

Parts of Speech

Write these words in the correct boxes.

meal	sharp	moan	squirm	garden
odd	worm	shrug	leaf	breakfast
scratch	wee	squeal	nice	yellow

Adjective	Noun	Verb
_____	_____	_____
_____	_____	_____
_____	_____	_____
_____	_____	_____
_____	_____	_____

Name _____

Six Little Chickens

Pretend there were six little chickens. Write a new verse for the poem.

Said the sixth little chicken

with a _____ _____ _____,

"I wish I could find

a _____ _____ _____."

Follow Directions

Draw six little chickens in the garden patch.
Draw what each chicken finds to eat.

Elf Owl

It's after dark in a desert of North America. A tiny predator silently swoops down and grabs a tasty insect. The tiny hunter is an elf owl.

The elf owl is the smallest owl in the world. It has yellow eyes and a yellow, brown, and gray body. Like larger owls, an elf owl is nocturnal. It searches for food at night and rests during the day.

An elf owl eats insects, scorpions, and small reptiles. Water is scarce in the desert. The little bird gets all the water it needs from its food. An elf owl is a smart hunter. It will grab the stalk of a plant and hang upside down from it. Then the elf owl beats its wings to make the stalk shake. Insects resting on the stalk run or fly and are caught by the hungry owl.

An elf owl often nests in holes left by other animals. Holes in saguaro cactuses are a favorite nesting place. In the spring, the female elf owl lays one to five tiny eggs in the nest. The male feeds the female while she sits on the eggs. He also brings food for her to give to the young owlets after they hatch.

Name _____

Questions about *Elf Owl*

1. What does an elf owl look like?

_____

2. Where do elf owls live?

_____

3. What do elf owls eat?

_____

4. How do elf owls get their food and water?

_____

5. Describe the nesting habits of elf owls.

_____

6. Why do you think the bird is called an **elf** owl?

_____

Think about It

Elf owls are predators. List eight predators.
Circle the bird names on your list.

_____   _____

_____   _____

_____   _____

_____   _____

Name _____

What Does It Mean?

Fill in the missing words.

1. A _____ animal looks for food at night and sleeps during the day.

2. Animals that hunt other animals for food are called _____.

3. Scaly animals like snakes and lizards are _____.

4. A young owl is called an _____.

5. Owl eggs crack when the babies are ready to _____.

6. Water is _____ in the desert.

7. The stem of a plant is its _____.

8. Elf owls _____ down and grab insects to eat.

| hatch | owlet | scarce | nocturnal |
| stalk | reptiles | swoop | predators |

Write one sentence using each of the following words to show you know its meaning.

cactus   desert   advantage

_____

_____

_____

Name _____

What Says er?

Circle the letters that say **er** in each of these words.

worm   skirt   purse   her   early

hunter   color   were   pearl   bird

Use the letters you circled to fill in the missing letters.

Owls are found all ov_____ the _____th. The tiny elf owl is the

smallest owl in the w_____ld. It is a predat_____. Aft_____ dark, this

noct_____nal animal comes out to hunt. An elf owl doesn't have to

w_____ry about getting th_____sty. It gets all the wat_____ it needs

from the food it eats.

Spell ô

The sound of **ô** is spelled in many ways.

tall   caught   bought   awful   soft

Circle the letter or letters that make the **ô** sound in these words.

call   taught   chalk   faucet   also

brought   often   author   watch   hawk

saw   across   moth   sought   caught

Base Word + Suffix

less means without   **ly** tells in what manner   **ful** means full of

Write the base word and add the correct suffix.

1. in a quick way   <u>quickly</u>
   base word + suffix

2. without harm   _____
   base word + suffix

3. in a silent way   _____
   base word + suffix

4. filled with fear   _____
   base word + suffix

5. without hope   _____
   base word + suffix

6. filled with joy   _____
   base word + suffix

Write one sentence using two of the new words you made.

_____

_____

Words into Syllables

A VCCV word is divided into syllables between the two consonants.

yellow   yel–low   insect   in–sect

Write the two syllables of each word.

1. cactus _____ _____   5. under _____ _____

2. sunny _____ _____   6. candle _____ _____

3. often _____ _____   7. upside _____ _____

4. into _____ _____   8. worry _____ _____

Name _____

As Small as an Elf Owl

An elf owl is about 6 inches (15 centimeters) tall. Cut out the ruler at the bottom of this page. Paste the two strips together. Measure objects until you find something about the same size as an elf owl.

List the items you measure. Use the back of this page if you need more room.

I measured these objects.	tall	wide
1.		
2.		
3.		
4.		
5.		
6.		
7.		
8.		

A _____ is about the same size as an elf owl.

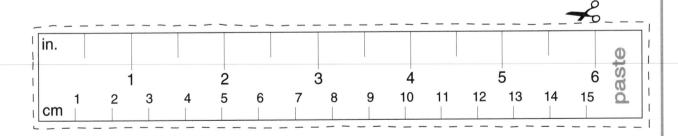

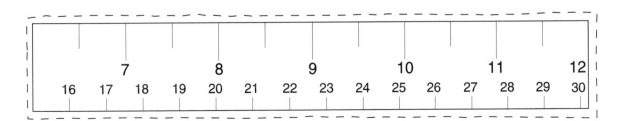

The Contest

Phyllis ran into the house waving the newspaper. "Fred, look at this. There's going to be a contest." The twins loved contests. They entered every one they could find. So far they hadn't won anything, but that didn't keep them from trying.

Groundhog Day was coming soon. It was a big day in the town where Phyllis and Fred lived. Every year the townspeople watched to see what happened when Phil, a local groundhog, came out of his hole. This year the newspaper was running a contest. People had to guess the time Phil would put in an appearance. The prize would be a trophy and a vacation to a warm, sunny place.

Phyllis and Fred hurried to the library to find out more about Groundhog Day. This is what they read:

Tradition says that groundhogs come out of their holes on February 2nd. If the groundhog comes out of his burrow and sees his shadow, he runs back into his burrow, and winter will last another six weeks. If the day is cloudy, the groundhog will not see his shadow. He will stay outside to wait for spring.

Next, Phyllis and Fred looked at old newspapers. They wanted to find out what time Phil had appeared in past years. They decided Phil would appear at 2:35 p.m. Phyllis telephoned the newspaper to enter their guess.

On February 2nd, the twins were up early. It wasn't easy, but they waited patiently to see when Phil would appear. At 2:35 p.m. the groundhog poked his nose out of his hole. He saw his shadow, and as quick as a wink, Phil disappeared back into his hole. Phyllis and Fred had won a contest!

Questions about *The Contest*

1. How did Phyllis find out about the contest?

   _____

2. What was the contest about?

   _____

3. What would the winner receive?

   _____

4. How did Phyllis and Fred prepare for the contest?

   _____

5. What is supposed to happen if:

   a. the groundhog sees its shadow? _____

   _____

   b. the groundhog does not see its shadow? _____

   _____

6. How do you think Phyllis and Fred would have felt if they lost the contest? Give a reason for your answer.

   _____

Think about It

On the back of this page, write about a contest you have entered. The contest could have taken place at school, at church, or at home. Describe the contest. Explain what you did to try to win. How did you feel when the contest was over?

What Does It Mean?

Find a word in the story that means:

1. a game or a race   _____

2. another name for a woodchuck   _____

3. beliefs, customs, or stories handed
   down from parents to children   _____

4. a prize, often in the shape of a
   statue or a cup, given to the winner
   of a contest   _____

5. two persons born at the same time
   to the same mother   _____

6. time for rest from school or work   _____

More Than One Meaning

What does **entered** mean in this story?
   a. went into a place
   b. joined a contest

What does **spring** mean in this story?
   a. the season after winter
   b. a small stream of water coming from the earth

What does **appearance** mean in this story?
   a. the way a person or thing looks
   b. coming into sight

What does **patient** mean in this story?
   a. waiting in a calm manner
   b. a person being treated by a doctor

Name _____

Spelling *f*

Both **f** and **ph** have the same sound.
Write the missing letters to name these pictures.

tele___one	___ence	go___er
tro___y	___inger	cal___

Contractions

Write the long form of each of the following contractions.
Fill in the boxes to find the secret word.

1. you've   y o u   h a̲ v e
                    3

2. there's   ___ ___ ___ ___ ___   ___ ___
                2

3. hadn't   ___ ___ ___   ___ ___ ___
               4

4. I've   ___   ___ ___ ___ ___

5. wasn't   ___ ___ ___   ___ ___ ___
               1

6. we'll   ___ ___   ___ ___ ___ ___
       6

7. won't   ___ ___ ___ ___   ___ ___ ___
                      5

8. it's   ___ ___   ___ ___

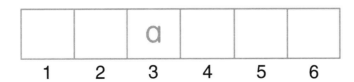

		a			
1	2	3	4	5	6

Name _____

Similes

Similes are figures of speech that compare two things in interesting or funny ways.

Match the parts of the following similes.

as quick	as a bug
as cute	as a mule
as mad	as a wink
as stubborn	as a mouse
as wise	as a wet hen
as quiet	as an owl

Write your own similes.

1. as strong as _____

2. as bright as _____

3. as soft as _____

4. as smooth as _____

What Happened Next?

Number the sentences in order.

___ Phyllis called the newspaper with a guess.

___ Phyllis found a contest in the newspaper.

___ Phil the groundhog came out of his hole at 2:35 p.m.

___ The twins won the contest.

___ Phyllis and Fred learned about Groundhog Day at the library.

Name _____

An Interview

A reporter from the newspaper is interviewing Phyllis and Fred after they won the contest. Write the answers you think they would give to the reporter's questions.

Reporter: "How do you feel about winning the contest?"

Phyllis: _____

_____

Fred: _____

_____

Reporter: "Where are you going on your vacation?"

Phyllis: _____

_____

Fred: _____

_____

Reporter: "Are you going to enter any more contests? Why?"

Phyllis: _____

_____

Fred: _____

_____

The Shark Lady

Do you know what you want to be when you grow up? Some people know when they are very young. Other people aren't sure until they are grown up. Eugenie Clark decided what she wanted to do when she was very young. She would study ocean fish, especially sharks.

Eugenie's father died when she was very young. Her mother had to work hard to support the family. Eugenie began to spend her Saturdays at the New York Aquarium. She would watch the fish for hours as they swam around in the large tanks. It felt like being a part of the sea. She loved the aquarium so much, she set up an aquarium at home.

The fish Eugenie loved the most were sharks. After watching them move back and forth in the tanks, she was eager to know more about them. How did their skin feel? What did they eat? How did they behave out in the ocean? These were only a few of the questions that filled her mind.

Eugenie studied hard and worked her way through college. She learned to dive so she could go down into the water and see sharks up close. She learned the answers to her questions as she observed the sharks.

Today Eugenie Clark, even in her 70s, is still studying ocean life. She goes down into the ocean in tiny submarines called submersibles. This allows her to study the unusual animal life in the dark depths of the ocean.

Eugenie Clark has spent her life doing what she loves best. Is there a career in your future waiting for you to do what you enjoy the most?

Questions about *The Shark Lady*

1. Where did Eugenie Clark spend her free time when she was a young girl?

   _____

2. How do you know she loved sea animals?

   _____

3. While she was in college, Eugenie learned to do something that was helpful in studying sharks. What was it?

   _____

4. How did Eugenie learn the answers to her questions about sharks?

   _____

5. What does she use now to go down into the dark depths of the ocean?

   _____

6. Why do you think Eugenie was given the nickname "Shark Lady"?

   _____

Think about It

Eugenie Clark was nicknamed "Shark Lady." What is your nickname? Who gave you the nickname? What does it mean?

_____

_____

_____

Name _____

What Does It Mean?

Find the words in the story that mean:

1. a place for showing collections of living water animals and plants _____

2. a large container for water _____

3. to learn more about something _____

4. watched closely _____

5. an occupation or a profession _____

6. a type of tiny submarine _____

7. deepest part of anything _____

8. time to come _____

Sharks

Find these sharks in the word search.

angel   frilled   mako   sevengill
blue   ✔hammerhead   megamouth   thresher
catshark   leopard   sawshark   whale

```
H A M M E R H E A D S M
T S U N A N B O G A E E
H T U N A K M L I N V G
R W H A L E O E U G E A
E S A L M O N O N E N M
S P E R C H O P T L G O
H X C A T S H A R K I U
E S A W S H A R K O L T
R F R I L L E D N D L H
```

Name _____

Aqua Means Water

Write **aqua** on the lines to make words. Draw a line from each word you
make to its meaning.

_____lung   an artificial pond or a tank for keeping water
                         plants and animals

_____naut
                         underwater breathing equipment

_____rium
                         in or on water

_____tic
                         an underwater explorer

Choose one of the words you made and use it in a sentence.

_____

_____

Sub Means Under

Write **sub** on the lines to make words. Draw a line from each word you make
to its meaning.

_____marine   underground

_____terranean   to go below the surface of the water

_____merge   a ship that can operate under the water

_____mersible   able to be submerged

Choose one of the words you made and use it in a sentence.

_____

_____

Name _____

When I Grow Up

Eugenie Clark knew she wanted to be a scientist and study sharks when she grew up. What do you want to become? Why do you want to do this?

_____

_____

_____

_____

Dr. Clark studied science and learned to dive. These helped her to become a scientist. What could you learn that will help you reach your goal?

_____

_____

_____

_____

Name _____

Name the Sharks

Sharks are often named after a physical characteristic. Look carefully at each shark shown here. Think about what each one looks like. Write the name of each shark on the line below it. Explain why the shark may have been given that name.

1

This is a _____.

It has _____

_____.

2

This is a _____.

It has _____

_____.

3

This is a _____.

It has _____

_____.

4

This is a _____.

It has _____

_____.

5

This is a _____.

It has _____

_____.

6
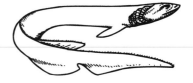

This is a _____.

It has _____

_____.

frilled shark	hammerhead shark	zebra shark
blacktip reef shark	Pacific angel shark	shortnose sawshark

Shadows

Have you ever played Shadow Tag with your friends? In Shadow Tag, the person who is "It" tries to step on another player's shadow. You need a big space outside so the players can run around without bumping into things. You have to play on a sunny day when shadows can be seen.

Do you know what makes a shadow? There has to be light. There also has to be something blocking the light. When you are outside during the day, light comes from the sun. If you block the sunlight, you will see a shadow on the other side of you.

Have you seen your shadow at different times of the day? Sometimes it looks long and skinny. At other times it looks short and fat. The size and shape of the shadow depends on where the sun is in the sky. If the sun is right overhead, a shadow will be short and fat. When the sun is lower in the sky, a shadow is long and skinny.

Have you ever been frightened by a strange shadow in your bedroom at night? What do you find if you turn on more lights? Anything that blocks light can make a shadow on your bedroom wall. Even after dark you can see shadows if there is a little light from a night-light or from moonlight shining through a window.

You can make your own shadows. Take a flashlight and shine it on a small object. Look past the object and you will see its shadow.

Name _____

Questions about *Shadows*

1. How do you play Shadow Tag?

_____

_____

2. What two things are needed to make a shadow?

_____

3. How do shadows change size and shape?

_____

4. How can there be a shadow at night?

_____

5. List four sources of light named in the story.

_____

Think about It

Circle **true** or **false**.

1. Shadows can change shape.	true	false
2. A shadow is the same size as the object making it.	true	false
3. Something must block light to make a shadow.	true	false
4. When the sun is overhead, a shadow is long and skinny.	true	false

Name _____

What Does It Mean?

Color in the circles to mark the word meanings.

In this story, the word **block** means:
○ a solid piece of wood, stone, metal, or ice
○ to keep something from passing through
○ an area in a city enclosed by four streets

In this story, the word **tag** means:
○ a piece of paper fastened to something
○ to follow closely behind someone
○ a children's game

In this story, the word **light** means:
○ the thing that lets us see more easily
○ not heavy
○ moving easily

In this story, the word **bump** means:
○ to collide with
○ to move along in jerks and bounces
○ an area raised above the surrounding surface

Use each word in a sentence to show you know its meaning.

shadow   frightened   night-light

1. _____

2. _____

3. _____

Long Vowel Sounds

Circle the letters in these words that make the long vowel sound.
Write the sound on the line.

1. shadow _____   6. light _____   11. paid _____

2. player _____   7. lower _____   12. strange _____

3. space _____   8. time _____   13. shine _____

4. outside _____   9. shape _____   14. know _____

5. seen _____   10. sky _____   15. night _____

Compound Words

Choose one word from each box to make a compound words.

out	any	some
over	bed	flash

room	light	side
thing	head	times

1. _____   4. _____

2. _____   5. _____

3. _____   6. _____

Write sentences using four of the compound words.

1. _____

2. _____

3. _____

4. _____

Make a Shadow

Draw the boy's shadow when the sun is in the position shown.

Name _____

Shadow Play

You will need:
    a flashlight
    a blank wall
    scissors
    2 sticks
    tape

1. Cut out the dragon and knight below.
2. Tape each picture to a stick.
3. Put the flashlight on a table. Point it at the wall. Turn on the flashlight.
4. Hold the stick puppets between the flashlight and the wall.
5. Tell a story.

Pecos Bill

Pecos Bill was the best cowboy in all of Texas. He could ride and rope better than anyone. Ridin' at a full gallop, Pecos could throw a rope around a whole herd of cattle. For all of his ropin', Pecos used the world's longest rattlesnake. Pecos Bill was a rough, tough customer. Why, he never lost a wrestlin' match, not even with a polecat or a grizzly bear.

When Bill was only five days old, his family headed west lookin' for a new homestead. He was ridin' in the back of his folks' covered wagon. Bill had been fussin' and cryin' since sunup. To shut him up, Bill's pa gave him a piece of fishing line with a hook. Bill dangled it in a river the wagon was passin' by. Before anyone knew what was happenin', Bill had hooked a catfish that weighed nigh on to a ton. Suddenly the catfish dived deep down into the river, pullin' little Bill out of the wagon. His folks didn't even notice he was gone.

Bill would have drowned, but a passin' coyote pulled him out of the water. The mother coyote picked Bill up by the scruff of his neck. She carried him to her den. Now Bill had four coyote brothers to play with. The mother coyote taught Bill the ways of wild creatures. He was a purty smart boy and soon learned how to move, hunt, and talk like a wild animal.

One day Bill was catchin' a nap in the shade of a tree, when a cowboy named Hank rode by. Hank was curious about the strange man restin' there. Hank asked Bill why he wasn't wearin' no clothes. "Coyotes don't wear clothes," answered Bill.

Hank almost fell off his horse, he was laughin' so hard. "You ain't no coyote. You're a Texan, just like me."

Well, Bill didn't take to that notion right off. He told Hank, "I have fleas like a coyote. I can howl like a coyote. I must be a coyote."

"Why, all the cowboys I know have fleas. And most of them howl at the moon once in a while. So that don't mean you're a coyote," said Hank. "I can prove you're not. Just come over here to the waterin' hole."

Hank pointed to Pecos Bill's reflection in the water. "You don't see no tail, do you? All coyotes have tails. Texas cowboys don't. Pardner, you are a cowboy!"

Bill couldn't argue with that, so he agreed to go with Hank. They set off for the nearest town. Hank gave Bill the extra clothes in his saddlebags. As they rode toward town, Hank began to teach Bill all he knew about being a cowboy.

Before long, folks were sayin', "What Pecos Bill don't know about bein' a cowboy ain't worth knowin'."

Name _____

Questions about *Pecos Bill*

1. How did baby Bill end up in the river?

_____

2. What did Bill learn from his coyote family?

_____

3. How did Hank convince Pecos Bill that he was not a coyote?

_____

4. What skills made Pecos Bill a great cowboy?

_____

5. What do these expressions mean?

   a. **it weighed nigh on to a ton** _____

   b. **he had a notion** _____

Think about It

A **cause** is an event that makes something else happen. The thing that happens is the **effect**. Fill in the missing cause and effect below.

Cause	Effect
_____ _____	Bill fell out of the wagon and into the river.
A coyote rescued Bill from the river and took him to her den.	_____ _____

Pecos Bill Crossword Puzzle

Word Box

cattle
coyote
curious
den
fleas
gallop
herd
hole
howl
notice
rope
saddlebags
Texan
ton

Across

2. eager to know
4. a group of large animals of one kind
6. a long, sad cry
7. fastest gait of a horse
8. a wild animal's home
11. a person from Texas
12. animals with hoofs, raised for meat and milk

Down

1. an open space in something solid
2. a wolflike animal
3. cases used to carry belongings on a horse
5. a strong, thick cord
9. to pay attention to
10. small, wingless insects that feed on blood
11. a weight of 2,000 pounds

Name _____

Silent Letters

Read the words. Cross out the letters that do not make a sound.

wrong	knee	talks	sign
climb	wrote	listen	know

Write the missing word or words in each sentence.

1. What is _____ with your bicycle?

2. It is important to _____ when your mother

   _____ to you.

3. Do you _____ what that street _____ says?

Long o

Long **o** is spelled many ways.

o   **o–e**   **ow**   **ew**   **oa**

Write the names of these long **o** pictures.

Name _____

Compound Words

Use the following words to make compound words.

cow   cat   saddle   rattle

fish   snake   boy   bags

1. _____   3. _____

2. _____   4. _____

Write a sentence using each new word you made. Circle the compound word in each sentence.

1. _____

2. _____

3. _____

4. _____

Homophones

Homophones are words that sound the same. They are not spelled the same and they have different meanings.

Circle the correct homophones.

1. I want to _____ how to use a computer.   no   know

2. The thief tried to _____ from the police.   flee   flea

3. Charlie's cat caught her long _____ in the door.   tale   tail

4. The ball went _____ Mr. Lee's shop window.   through   threw

5. Holly _____ a letter to her pen pal in Mexico.   scent   sent

Pecos Bill

Pecos Bill is a "tall tale." Tall tales are filled with exaggeration, telling things that could never happen in real life.

Write three events from the story that could happen.

_____

_____

_____

Write three events that could not really happen.

_____

_____

_____

■ ■

Pecos Bill was written as though it were being told by someone who had not spent much time in school. There are words with missing letters, and there are sentences without proper grammar.

Copy these sentences. Correct the spelling and language.

1. Bill had been fussin' and cryin' since sunup.

_____

2. You ain't no coyote.

_____

3. You don't see no tail, do you?

_____

4. What Pecos Bill don't know about bein' a cowboy ain't worth knowin'.

_____

Cactus—A Desert Plant

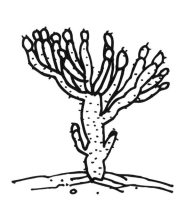  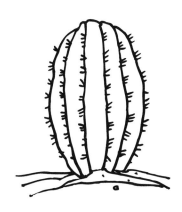

The plants of the desert are good at surviving drought. They must be able to go without water for a long time. Cactuses are one kind of plant that can grow in these hot, dry regions.

Cactuses look different from each other, but they are all alike in one way—they can store water. The water is gathered by roots and carried to the plant, where it is stored. Cactuses have thick stems. They are usually covered in thorns or spines instead of leaves. They have hairy fuzz that helps prevent water loss.

A cholla cactus has spines as sharp as needles. It is the desert's most prickly cactus. The spines come off the cactus so easily they seem to jump at passersby. Pack rats pile up prickly cholla stems at the entrances to their burrows. The stems protect their homes from invaders.

A saguaro is a tall, treelike cactus with a thick stem. It has branches that reach upward. The stem is pleated like an accordion. It can store huge amounts of water. The cactus has waxy white flowers that are followed by red fruits.

A barrel cactus is fat and round like the barrel it is named after. It is covered with spines. Thousands of roots spread out in a wide circle just under the ground where it grows. The roots absorb water and take it to the barrel above ground. Like the saguaro, its accordion-pleated sides stretch to store water. The cactus shrinks as the water is used up.

There are many other types of cactuses growing in the deserts of North America. Each kind of cactus has special ways to store water.

Pronunciation Key

saguaro—sə wä´ rō　　cholla—choi´ ə

Name _____

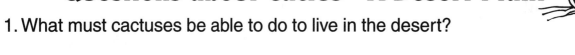

Questions about *Cactus—A Desert Plant*

1. What must cactuses be able to do to live in the desert?

   _____

2. What do cactuses have instead of flat leaves?

   _____

3. How are all cactuses alike?

   _____

4. Name the cactus that:

   a. is as tall as a tree   _____

   b. is fat and round   _____

   c. has the prickliest spines of any cactus   _____

5. How do accordion-pleated sides help a cactus survive?

   _____

Think about It

A lot of desert plants have imaginative names. When you hear them, you might get a funny picture in your mind. Name these unusual cactuses.

Old Man Cactus   **Peanut Cactus**   **Bunny Ears**

_____   _____   _____

Name _____

Cactus Crossword Puzzle

Word Box

absorb
accordion
cactus
desert
drought
prevent
saguaro
spines
stem
store
survive
thorns

Across
4. back-and-forth folds
6. main part of a cactus above ground
7. sharp points on a stem
9. to put away to use later
10. a region with little or no water
11. to remain alive

Down
1. to take in or soak up
2. a long time without rain
3. a type of tall cactus
5. a desert plant usually having spines
6. stiff, pointed growths on plants
8. to keep from happening

Name _____

Sounds of c

Write the sound made by the underlined **c** in these words.

1. ca̲ctus _____   5. produc̲e _____   9. penc̲il _____

2. c̲arried _____   6. acc̲ordion _____   10. c̲ustard _____

3. c̲ircle _____   7. c̲ity _____   11. onc̲e _____

4. surfac̲e _____   8. c̲ut _____   12. c̲ircus _____

Which vowels usually follow the "s" sound of **c**? _____

Which vowels usually follow the "k" sound of **c**? _____

More Than One

Add **s** or **es** to each word to make more than one.

1. cactus _____   4. branch _____

2. desert _____   5. ditch _____

3. drought _____   6. plant _____

Some words have special spellings for more than one.

woman _____   ox _____   mouse _____

Fill in the plural forms of the words you wrote to complete these sentences.

1. Six gray _____ were hiding under the sink.

2. All of the _____ were wearing hats with flowers.

3. A team of six _____ pulled the covered wagon.

Name _____

Saguaro Cactus—Oak Tree

Make a ✔ when the fact is true.

	saguaro cactus	oak tree
1. has spines	✔	
2. has flat leaves		
3. has roots that absorb water		
4. is tall		
5. has accordion-pleated sides		
6. has seeds called acorns		
7. lives in a forest		
8. lives in a desert		

Find the Cactus

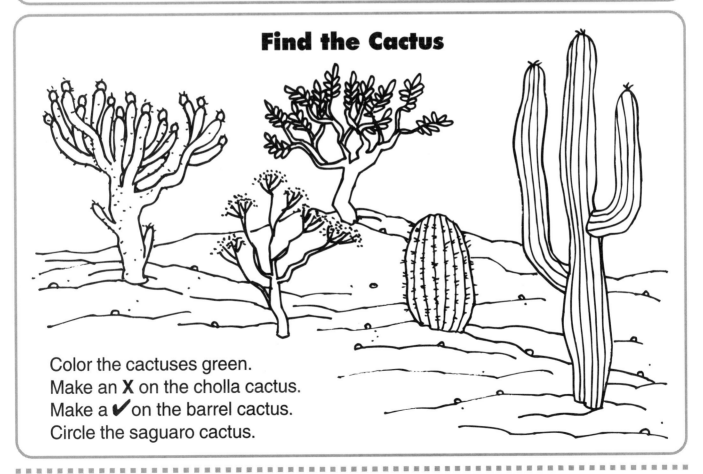

Color the cactuses green.
Make an **X** on the cholla cactus.
Make a ✔ on the barrel cactus.
Circle the saguaro cactus.

Name _____

A Cactus Report

Go to the library and find out more about cactuses. Write a paragraph about what you learn.

I read _____.
(title of book, magazine, or encyclopedia)

This is what I learned:	Draw a cactus.
_____	
_____	
_____	
_____	
_____	
_____	
_____	
_____	
_____	
_____	
_____	
_____	
_____	
_____	

Orangutans

Orangutans are tree-dwelling apes. They live in tropical forests in Asia. They are found in the wild in only two places—the islands of Borneo and Sumatra.

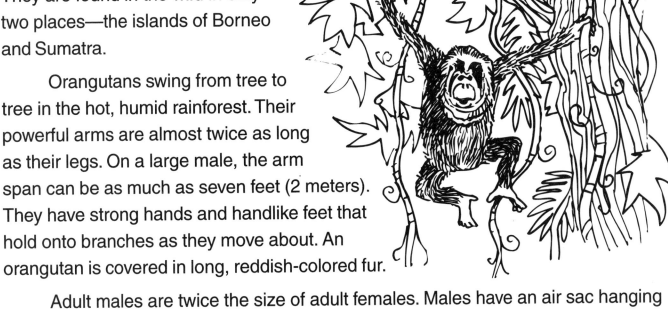

Orangutans swing from tree to tree in the hot, humid rainforest. Their powerful arms are almost twice as long as their legs. On a large male, the arm span can be as much as seven feet (2 meters). They have strong hands and handlike feet that hold onto branches as they move about. An orangutan is covered in long, reddish-colored fur.

Adult males are twice the size of adult females. Males have an air sac hanging down from their throats. This air sac can be inflated and used to make a loud call. The call can be heard at great distances in the forest.

Orangutans in the wild eat more than 400 different foods. The greatest part of their diet is fruit and tender, young plant leaves. They also eat other tree parts, honey, termites, and fungi.

Young orangutans remain with their mothers for about eight years. During the day, the females and their young travel in small groups looking for food. The young orangutans learn how to forage for food by observing their mothers. Males generally live alone and are very territorial.

At night orangutans place branches and leaves in the forks of trees to build sleeping platforms.

Orangutans are endangered animals. Farming and timber harvesting are taking over their rainforest habitat. Orangutans are also illegally hunted. The captured orangutans are sold to zoos and circuses. When young orangutans are rescued, they must be taught how to climb trees and how to find food. If they can learn these skills, they can be returned to the forest.

Name _____

Questions about *Orangutans*

1. Describe an orangutan.

   _____

2. What is unusual about the arms of an orangutan? How does this help
   the animal?

   _____

3. What are the main foods eaten by an orangutan?

   _____

4. What does a young orangutan learn from its mother? How does it learn?

   _____

5. What does a male orangutan use to make loud noises?

   _____

6. What is the difference in size between male and female orangutans?

   _____

7. Why are orangutans endangered?

   _____

8. What do you think will happen to the wild orangutan in the future?
   Give a reason for your answer.

   _____

   _____

Think about It

Young orangutans learn from their mothers. On the back of this page,
describe one thing you have learned from your mother. How did you
learn it?

What Does It Mean?

Match each word to its meaning.

1. tropical   against the law

2. arm span   moist; damp

3. observe   hot, humid

4. illegal   greatest distance between
                               the fingertips of your two hands

5. humid
                               to fill with air

6. forage
                               to watch or to notice

7. inflate
                               to search for food

In this story:

1. **greatest** means
   a. the largest amount
   b. the biggest ape
   c. the most important

2. **leaves** means
   a. goes away
   b. lets alone
   c. thin, flat green parts of a plant

3. **part** means
   a. a section of the whole thing
   b. a dividing line left when the hair is combed
   c. a part in a play

Name _____

Where Do You Hear *o*?

Circle the words that have the long **o** sound.

1. alone	5. stout	9. mower	13. know
2. Borneo	6. open	10. hello	14. of
3. flower	7. whole	11. stone	15. coat
4. throat	8. foam	12. come	16. grow

Write the long **o** words in the correct boxes.

o—e	open syllable	oa	ow

The Sounds of *ed*

Write each word under the sound made by **ed**.

ed	d	t

picked	suited	begged	wanted	returned	raked
hunted	wished	covered	inflated	looked	colored

Name _____

Synonyms—Antonyms

Synonyms are words that have about the same meaning.
Antonyms are words that have opposite meanings.
Make an **X** on the pairs of synonyms. Circle the pairs of antonyms.

female–male   forage–hunt

twice–double   build–construct

large–small   arid–humid

capture–catch   powerful–strong

same–different   dwelling–living

teach–learn   old–young

How Many Syllables?

Write the number of syllables in each word.

1. wild ___1___   6. adult _____   11. relocation _____

2. islands _____   7. branches _____   12. observing _____

3. orangutan _____   8. illegally _____   13. different _____

4. Borneo _____   9. habitat _____   14. generally _____

5. Sumatra _____   10. rescued _____   15. strong _____

Name _____

Create a poster about the endangered orangutan.

Save the Orangutan

Answer Key

Page 5
1. Mother sent the children outdoors because they were being too noisy.
2. The children put on snow boots, jackets, earmuffs, gloves, and scarves.
3. You wear a scarf around your neck. You wear earmuffs on your ears.
4. They had a snowball fight. Jay made snowmen. Joy made snow angels.
5. Joy, Jay, Mother, and Grandpa went for a sleigh ride.
6. Everyone was bundled up in warm clothes. OR It started to snow again.

Page 6
1. scarf
2. wrap
3. wool
4. earmuffs
5. sleigh

settle down–be still and quiet
all bundled up–wearing a lot of warm clothes

1. earmuffs
2. scarf
3. jacket
4. gloves
5. snow boots

Page 7
snowfl<u>a</u>ke   sl<u>eigh</u>   p<u>ai</u>nt
c<u>a</u>ke   r<u>ai</u>n   <u>eigh</u>t

up—down   happy—jolly
large—big   play—work
fast—speedy   tiny—little
noisy—quiet   front—back
indoors—outside   night—day

Page 8
1. they
2. it
3. he
4. we
5. her
6. them

1. shouted   4. ate
2. ran   5. began
3. played   6. made

1. played
2. make
3. began

Page 9
1. playing   played
2. painting   painted
3. pulling   pulled

1. tugging   tugged
2. zipping   zipped
3. wrapping   wrapped

1. moving   1. moved
2. exciting   2. excited
3. smiling   3. smiled

Sentences will vary.

Page 11
1. Rama had new blue shoes.
2. Rama's shoe was missing.
3. She looked under her bed and around the bedroom.
4. Her little sister would have taken both shoes. Her brother had spent the night at a friend's house.
5. Rama saw dirty paw prints going out of her room.
6. She was unhappy. OR She was upset.
7. Answers will vary, but could include:
   Mother will take the shoe to be fixed.
   Mother will buy Rama a new pair of shoes.
   Rama will clean up the shoe and wear it just the way it is.

Page 12
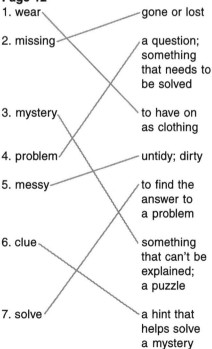
1. wear — to have on as clothing
2. missing — gone or lost
3. mystery — something that can't be explained; a puzzle
4. problem — a question; something that needs to be solved
5. messy — untidy; dirty
6. clue — a hint that helps solve a mystery
7. solve — to find the answer to a problem

1. foot
2. shoe or blue or clue
3. right

1. two
2. too
3. to

Page 13
sh<u>oe</u>s   bl<u>ue</u>   f<u>ew</u>
sch<u>oo</u>l   b<u>oo</u>t   tw<u>o</u>
n<u>ew</u>   wh<u>o</u>   cl<u>ue</u>

sh<u>oe</u>s   b<u>oo</u>t   tw<u>o</u>

1. foot   5. swim
2. out   6. color
3. eat   7. king
4. green   8. hive

Page 14
Rama got new blue shoes with silver buckles.
One of Rama's new blue shoes was missing.
Her little sister did not take the shoe.
Her brother did not take the shoe.
Rama found a clue. It was a dirty paw print.
Rama found the missing shoe in Sofie's doghouse.

Page 17
1. The crow thought he was handsome and could sing better than anyone.
2. The crow flew up to a fence and started to eat.
3. The fox thought he would like the cheese.
4. The fox flattered the crow. OR The fox asked to hear the crow's beautiful voice.
5. Answers will vary, but could include:
   crow—vain, beautiful, stupid
   fox—clever, tricky, hungry
6. The crow learned not to trust a flatterer.

Page 18

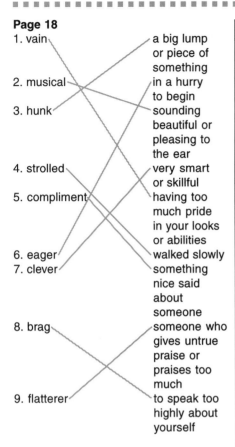

1. vain — having too much pride in your looks or abilities
2. musical — sounding beautiful or pleasing to the ear
3. hunk — a big lump or piece of something
4. strolled — walked slowly
5. compliment — something nice said about someone
6. eager — in a hurry to begin
7. clever — very smart or skillful
8. brag — to speak too highly about yourself
9. flatterer — someone who gives untrue praise or praises too much

fox   crow

Page 19

a	e	i	o	u
aunt	held	with	drop	hunk
have	fell	pick	fox	such
dance	met	trick	bought	come
ran	best	hymn	bottle	of

the ~~the~~
they ~~they~~
thousand ~~thousand~~
thick ~~thick~~

these ~~these~~
thorns ~~thorns~~
thing ~~thing~~
there ~~there~~

three ~~three~~
that ~~that~~
weather ~~weather~~
with ~~with~~

Page 20

1. picked   picking
   started   starting

2. dropped   dropping
   grabbed   grabbing

3. hurried
   studied

4. hurrying
   studying

1. dropped   started
2. grabbed   hurried

Page 21

walk   stroll   pick   flew
heard   thought   think   when
fence   cheese   ask   grab
open   bright   hungry   fox
called   swoop   sit   brag

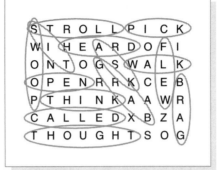

S T R O L L P I C K
W I H E A R D O F I
O N T O G S W A L K
O P E N R R K C E B
P T H I N K A A W R
C A L L E D X B Z A
T H O U G H T S O G

1. picked   flew
2. strolled   saw
3. opened   fell
4. thought   make   drop
5. grabbed   gobbled

Page 24

1. Dad's idea was to take a vacation.
2. They went to visit Aunt Myrtle. OR They went to the beach.
3. The pet sitter was late and they had a flat tire.
4. Dad went fishing.
   Mom read a book at the beach.
   David went surfing with his cousins.
   Rosie took pictures at the beach.
   Tony built a sand castle and found hermit crabs.
5. You keep a diary to write down how you feel and what you did.

Solution—Dad said Tony could sit by the window first.
Problem—The car had a flat tire.

Page 25

1. diary — a book in which you write down what happens each day
2. beach — a shore area of sand or pebbles along the ocean
3. alarm — a bell or other device to warn or waken people
4. middle — halfway between; in the center
5. vending machine — a machine from which you get candy, stamps, or other objects when money is dropped in
6. luggage — suitcases or other bags carried by a traveler
7. shallow — not deep
8. sitter — a person who watches someone's children, pets, or belongings

hermit crab   sailboat   whale

Page 26

drive   cry   sight   write
night   lie   sky   pie

1. flying
2. fighting
3. idea
4. tire

1. great
2. to/two
3. we
4. need
5. sea
6. read
7. some
8. wait

Sentences will vary.

Page 27
1. excited OR happy
2. angry OR upset
3. calm OR happy
4. impatient OR upset
5. thankful OR relieved

2
5
1
4
3

Page 29
1. Butter was a small, round, yellow hen.
2. Butter wanted to hatch some eggs. OR Butter was ready to be a mother.
3. The farmer didn't want any more chickens.
4. The farmer thought a hawk or a fox caught Butter.
5. She laid eggs and hatched them while she was gone.
6. Answers will vary, but could include:
   The chicks were cute.
   He decided he could use more hens after all.
   He didn't want to take the chicks away from their mother.

Page 30
1. clever — smart
2. disappear — to go out of sight; vanish
3. dozen — 12 of anything
4. hatch — to break out of an egg
5. chuckle — to laugh
6. gently — kindly; carefully
7. stubborn — won't give up
8. coop — a pen for chickens

Page 31
ow in now	o in crow
brown	blow
crowd	flown
tower	follow
allow	own
flower	tow
clown	sown

parts of a bird	animal homes
feather	coop
beak	✔garage
claws	barn
✔hair	sty

chicken family
hen
chick
✔goose
rooster

Page 32
1. small   6. sat
2. day   7. mother
3. take   8. found
4. more   9. lived
5. couldn't   10. disappeared

(yellow) large (stubborn)
lazy (round) (small)
(busy) (clever) tall
Sentences will vary.

Page 33
Butter laid a little brown egg almost every day.
Butter began to sit on the eggs in her nest.
The farmer took the eggs out of Butter's nest.
The farmer could not find Butter. She had disappeared.
Butter came back, followed by three tiny, fluffy chicks.

Page 35
1. Used clothes were in the box.
2. A vest (or denim overalls) was in the box.
3. Ginny didn't want to wear Peggy's old clothes again. OR Ginny wanted some new clothes.
4. The locket was handed down from Ginny's grandmother to her mother.
5. Answers will vary, but could include:
   The clothes were still good.
   Peggy liked to share with Ginny.
   Peggy had outgrown the clothes and thought Ginny would like them.

Page 36
1. precious
2. great-grandmother
3. cousin
4. denim
5. hand-me-downs
6. huge

overalls   vest   locket

Page 37
1. j   5. j   9. g
2. j   6. g   10. j
3. g   7. j   11. j
4. g   8. g   12. g

1. hug
2. locket
3. vest
4. cousin
5. clothes
6. year
7. new/you
8. wear
9. mother
10. see

Page 38
clothing web	jewelry web
overalls	watch
coat	ring
vest	pin
shirt	locket
sweater	bracelet
pants	necklace

relatives

Page 42
1. The prince had to marry a real princess.
2. The prince went to his mother for advice.
3. She placed a small dried pea under a pile of mattresses. Women wanting to marry the prince had to sleep on the mattresses.
4. The queen thought a real princess was so delicate she would feel the pea while she slept.
5. The bedraggled girl was a real princess.
6. Answers will vary.

Page 43
1. bride — a woman just married or to be married
2. kingdom — a country governed by a king or a queen
3. advice — an idea about what should be done
4. delicate — easily hurt and needing special care
5. lump — a small, solid hunk
6. bedchamber — a room for sleeping
7. mattress — a thick pad used for a bed
8. bedraggled — wet and untidy

sweet dreams–have a good sleep
soaking wet–wet all the way to
your skin

<u>un</u>comfortable   <u>un</u>happy
<u>un</u>married   <u>un</u>able

Sentences will vary.

Page 44

1. o	6. e	11. a
2. i	7. i	12. e
3. e	8. u	13. u
4. o	9. a	14. a
5. i	10. u	15. o

1. dreams	5. princesses
2. mattresses	6. coaches
3. peas	7. stories
4. berries	8. kingdoms

1. women	3. geese
2. children	4. men

Page 45
1. Problem—Sherry had to earn half
the money for the new bike she
wanted.
Solution—She did jobs in the
neighborhood. OR She baby-sat,
mowed lawns, and ran errands.
2. Problem—Harry had weak
muscles. He couldn't walk or pick
up things.
Solution—Harry used an electric
wheelchair. He had a special dog
that picked up things for him.

Page 46
3
2
6
4
5
1
7

1. happy
2. excited
3. unhappy OR disappointed
4. happy

Page 49
1. Peter was a boy.
Thomas was a mouse.
2. Thomas lived in a hole in the wall
of Peter's bedroom.
3. Thomas bumped the switch and
turned on the computer.
He jumped onto the keyboard and
pressed the keys.
4. They peeked in the door to see

who was touching the computer.
5. Dad was making a joke because
a computer has a mouse and
Thomas was a mouse that got
on the computer.
6. Answers will vary.

Page 50
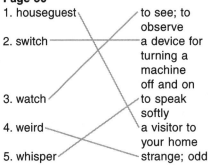
1. houseguest   to see; to
                       observe
2. switch   a device for
                       turning a
                       machine
                       off and on
3. watch   to speak
                       softly
4. weird   a visitor to
                       your home
5. whisper   strange; odd

mouse—a computer tool and
a small animal
off he shot like a rocket—he
moved quickly

Sentences will vary.

Page 51

m<u>ou</u>se	br<u>ow</u>n	h<u>ou</u>r
fr<u>ow</u>n	n<u>ow</u>	f<u>ou</u>nd
<u>ou</u>t	h<u>ou</u>se	h<u>ow</u>
sh<u>ou</u>t	d<u>ow</u>n	r<u>ou</u>nd

T~~h~~omas	lis~~t~~en	~~K~~now
~~W~~rite	ta~~l~~k	si~~g~~n

1. wrote	3. listened
2. knew	4. talked

Page 56
1. They are leprechauns.
2. He was taking the potatoes from
Sean O'Toole's farm.
3. He was taking them. OR He was
stealing them.
4. Paddy needed help to pull out the
giant potato.
5. Sean O'Toole was very upset. He
chased the leprechauns out of
his field.
6. Paddy used leprechaun magic.

Page 57

1. leprechaun	5. spied
2. field	6. scoundrels
3. borrow	7. escaped
4. delicious	

Sentences will vary.

Page 58

children	potatoes
noises	
bushes	
leaves	
bunnies	

I will	will not
we will	should not
they will	have not
will	not

he is	we have
there is	they have
it is	I have
is	have

Page 62
1. It flew at night.
2. A bat uses echoes.
3. fly, swoop, dive
4. The bat eats insects.
5. The bat sleeps in a cave.
6. Bats are helpful because they
eat insects.

Page 63

1. echoes	4. cave	7. ceiling
2. swoop	5. nearby	
3. snug	6. guide	

1. ceiling
2. through
3. toes

1. threw	through
2. sealing	ceiling
3. toes	tows

Page 64
night—flight OR tight
nearby—fly OR sky
Other words will vary.

light	**end**
1. fight	1. mend
2. right	2. bend
3. tight	3. lend
4. night	4. send
5. flight	5. tend
6. fright	6. blend
7. sight	7. spend

Page 65

1. i	6. i
2. e	7. i
3. i	8. e
4. e	9. e
5. e	10. i

end of a one-syllable word—i
end of a two-syllable word—e

one syllable	two syllables
night	furry
guide	listen
wrapped	echo
warm	little
swamp	nearby
cave	sleepy
through	insect

Page 66

Order will vary, but should include:
uses echoes as a guide
comes out at night
eats insects
catches insects while flying
lives in a cave
uses toes to hang onto the ceiling
of the cave
wraps wings around its body as
it sleeps
sleeps during the day

Page 69

1. Bats can fly.
2. A bat's wing is made of muscle, bone, and skin. It has bones a lot like a hand.
3. A bat uses its tail for balance and making turns.
4. A bat uses its claws to hold onto the ceiling when it sleeps.
5. A bat makes a sound and then listens for the echo that bounces off things.
6. They eat millions of insects that could destroy crops. OR They help spread pollen.
7. Answers will vary, but could include:
   Insects would eat up all the crops. There wouldn't be as many plants growing.

Answers will vary, but should include some of the following:
Same—Bats and birds both have wings. Some bats and birds eat insects. Some bats and birds eat plant seeds.

Different—Birds have feathers. Bats have fur.
Birds lay eggs. Bats have live babies.
Most birds look for food during the day. Most bats look for food at night.

Page 70

1. surroundings — things or conditions around you
2. attic — a space in a house just below the roof and above the other rooms
3. destroy — to spoil or ruin
4. crops — plants grown to be used by people
5. rodents — a group of animals with large front teeth used for gnawing; rats, mice, squirrels
6. mammal — a warm-blooded animal whose babies drink milk from the mother's body
7. balanced — in a steady position
8. colonies — groups of bats living together

insect-eating bat   fruit-eating bat

Page 71

~~eating~~   ~~eagle~~   ~~seeds~~   ~~leaf~~
as~~lee~~p   ~~tree~~s   ~~queen~~   ~~clean~~
jelly b~~ea~~n   ~~cree~~p   ~~dream~~   ~~feet~~

1. jelly b<u>ea</u>ns
2. <u>ea</u>gle   tr<u>ee</u>s
3. <u>ea</u>ting   s<u>ee</u>ds
4. Cl<u>ea</u>n   f<u>ee</u>t
5. qu<u>ee</u>n   asl<u>ee</u>p   dr<u>ea</u>m

~~collar~~   ~~work~~   ~~color~~   ~~earth~~   ~~her~~   ~~third~~   ~~purse~~

1. doct<u>or</u>s   n<u>ur</u>ses   w<u>or</u>ked
   aft<u>er</u>   <u>ear</u>thquake
2. Moth<u>er</u>   h<u>er</u>   p<u>ear</u>l
   Sat<u>ur</u>day
3. out<u>er</u>   c<u>ur</u>ve   <u>ear</u>th
4. humming b<u>ir</u>d   nect<u>ar</u>   flow<u>er</u>

Page 72

Answers will vary, but should include some of the following:

insect-eating bat
eats insects
uses echolocation
has big ears
has good hearing
both
can fly
come out at night
covered in fur
mammals
live babies
fruit-eating bat
small ears
eats fruit and flowers
spreads pollen and seeds
has a good sense of smell

Page 73

1. fact	5. opinion
2. opinion	6. fact
3. fact	7. opinion
4. fact	8. fact

1. better	6. under
2. smaller	7. female
3. catch	8. curved
4. live	9. find
5. sleeping	10. destroy

Page 74

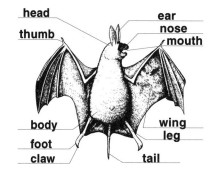

head
ear
nose
mouth
thumb
body
wing
leg
foot
claw
tail

Page 77

1. A thieving animal was stealing the farmer's corn.
2. The farmer planned to have one of his sons stop the animal.
3. He promised to give all he owned to the son who stopped the animal.
4. The toad told each brother he would need to listen to him if he planned to catch the thief.
5. The thief never came while the oldest son was there.
6. The second son shot the bird but only knocked off some of its feathers.

                   More Read and Understand • Grade 3 • EMC 747

7. The youngest son saw a bird. The toad stopped him from shooting the bird, because it was really a girl.
8. They were jealous because Carlos got a wife and all that their father owned.

Page 78

1. thief — a person who steals
2. destroy — to ruin something or make it useless
3. boast — to speak too highly about yourself
4. appear — to come into sight
5. realize — to understand clearly
6. dusk — the time just before dark
7. trudged — walked tiredly
8. task — work to be done
9. bewitched — under a spell

well—a source of water
change—to become different

Page 79

thief happy seen she
three he plead lazy
field keep breathe street
deep believe squeal

1. younger	youngest
2. lazier	laziest
3. tinier	tiniest
4. deeper	deepest
5. richer	richest
6. happier	happiest

Sentences will vary.

Page 80

an old farmer	an orange	a well
an animal	an alligator	an egg
a cornfield	a frog	an angel
a large bird	an insect	a feather

Maryanne	bedroom
blackbirds	cornfield
dishpan	into
scarecrow	afternoon
maybe	

Page 81

	Miguel	Luis	Carlos
boastful	✓	✓	
kind			✓
liar		✓	
unkind	✓	✓	
jealous	✓	✓	
honest			✓
eager	✓	✓	✓
successful			✓

Answers will vary, but they could include:
Could really happen...
A farmer could have a cornfield.
Animals could eat the corn.
A farmer could send his sons to stop the animal.
The sons could shoot at the bird.

Couldn't happen...
A toad can't talk.
A stone can't grant wishes.
A witch can't turn a girl into a bird.
A bird can't change into a girl.

Page 84

1. She heard a noise when she stopped to tie a shoelace.
2. The dog was in an alley among the garbage.
3. The dog's ribs were sticking out. OR The dog was very skinny.
4. Rita brought the dog food and water.
5. One day the dog came up to Rita and let her pet him.
6. They took the dog to the vet to see if he was sick or injured.
7. Answers will vary, but should include the idea that the dog trusted or loved Rita.
8. Answers will vary.

Page 85

1. alley — a narrow street in the middle of a city block
2. whimper — to whine; a complaining cry
3. skinny — very thin
4. crept — moved slowly with body close to the ground
5. kindness — gentleness; helpfulness
6. leftovers — food left after a meal
7. vet — a short name for a doctor who treats animals

Page 86

though fought tough
Sentences will vary.

1. f	6. f
2. silent	7. f
3. silent	8. silent
4. f	9. f
5. silent	10. silent

Page 87

Cause—Rita heard a noise that sounded like a dog whimpering coming from the alley.
Effect—The dog began to trust Rita. OR The dog let Rita pet him. OR The dog followed Rita home.

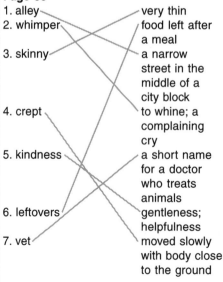

"Dog" is in the word search 5 times.

Page 89

1. first chicken—worm
   second chicken—slug
   third chicken—meal
   fourth chicken—leaf
   fifth chicken—gravel stone
2. A gravel stone helps a chicken grind up its food.
3. Mother told the little chickens to scratch in the garden.
4. It took place in the morning. It was breakfast time, and you eat breakfast in the morning.
5. Answers will vary.

Page 90

1. odd	5. moan
2. garden	6. faint
3. stone/gravel	7. sigh
4. meal	8. scratch

Page 86 (continued)

1. slowly 5. thoughtful
2. hopeful 6. harmless
3. careful 7. sadly
4. homeless 8. careless

1. strange little squirm
2. sharp little squeal
3. faint little moan
4. odd little shrug
5. fat little worm
6. little green leaf
7. nice yellow meal

Page 91
1. <u>ch</u>ickens scra<u>tch</u> <u>patch</u>
2. rea<u>ch</u> pea<u>ch</u> bran<u>ch</u>
3. wa<u>tch</u> <u>ch</u>ain
4. ben<u>ch</u> wa<u>tch</u>ed bea<u>ch</u>

squirm—worm meal—squeal
shrug—slug grief—leaf
patch—scratch stone—moan

1. worm
2. squeal
3. slug leaf
4. moan

Page 92
second little chicken
fifth little chicken
the mother
first little chicken
fourth little chicken
the mother
third little chicken

Adjective	Noun	Verb
odd	meal	scratch
sharp	worm	squirm
wee	garden	shrug
nice	breakfast	moan
yellow	leaf	squeal

Page 95
1. An elf owl is small with yellow eyes and a yellow, brown, and gray body.
2. They live in the deserts of North America.
3. Elf owls eat insects, scorpions, and small reptiles.
4. They swoop down and grab their prey. OR They shake the stalk of a plant to make insects fly off. They get water from the food they eat.
5. Elf owls lay their eggs in holes left by other animals. OR Elf owls nest in holes in saguaro cactus. The female sits on the eggs. The male brings food for the female and the owlets.
6. It is called an elf owl because it is small and an elf is small.

Page 96
1. nocturnal
2. predators
3. reptiles
4. owlet
5. hatch
6. scarce
7. stalk
8. swoop

Sentences will vary.

Page 97
w<u>or</u>m sk<u>ir</u>t p<u>ur</u>se h<u>er</u> <u>ear</u>ly
hunt<u>er</u> col<u>or</u> w<u>er</u>e p<u>ear</u>l b<u>ir</u>d

<u>over</u> <u>earth</u>
w<u>or</u>ld predat<u>or</u> After
noct<u>ur</u>nal
w<u>or</u>ry th<u>ir</u>sty wat<u>er</u>

c(a)ll acr(o)ss w(a)tch
br(ou)ght ch(a)lk s(ou)ght
s(aw) (au)thor (a)lso
t(au)ght m(o)th h(aw)k
(o)ften f(au)cet c(au)ght

Page 98
1. quickly
2. harmless
3. silently
4. fearful
5. hopeless
6. joyful

Sentences will vary.

1. cac tus 4. in to 7. up side
2. sun ny 5. un der 8. wor ry
3. of ten 6. can dle

Sentences will vary.

Page 101
1. Phyllis read about the contest in the newspaper.
2. People were to guess the time the groundhog would come out of its hole on Groundhog Day.
3. The winner would get a trophy and a vacation to a sunny place.
4. Phyllis and Fred went to the library to find out when the groundhog had come out in past years.
5. a. If the groundhog sees its shadow, it goes back into its hole, and there is six more weeks of winter.
   b. If the groundhog doesn't see its shadow, spring is here.
6. Answers will vary.

Page 102
1. contest
2. groundhog
3. tradition
4. trophy
5. twins
6. vacation

entered—b appearance—b
spring—a patient—a

Page 103
telephone fence gop<u>h</u>er
tro<u>ph</u>y finger cal<u>f</u>

1. you have 4. I have 7. will not
2. there is 5. was not 8. it is
3. had not 6. we will

shadow

Page 104
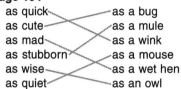
as quick → as a wink
as cute → as a mouse
as mad → as a wet hen
as stubborn → as a mule
as wise → as a bug
as quiet → as an owl

Answers will vary.

3
1
4
5
2

Page 107
1. She spent her free time in the New York Aquarium.
2. She watched them all the time. OR She set up an aquarium at home. OR She spent her life studying them.
3. Eugenie learned to dive.
4. Eugenie learned the answers to her questions by observing sharks in the ocean.
5. She uses a tiny submarine called a submersible.
6. She got her nickname because she liked sharks so much. OR She got her nickname because she studied sharks.

Page 108
1. aquarium 5. career
2. tank 6. submersible

Page 109

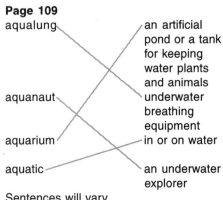

aqualung — underwater breathing equipment

aquanaut — an underwater explorer

aquarium — an artificial pond or a tank for keeping water plants and animals

aquatic — in or on water

Sentences will vary.

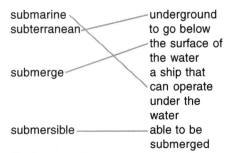

submarine — a ship that can operate under the water

subterranean — underground

submerge — to go below the surface of the water

submersible — able to be submerged

Sentences will vary.

Page 111

1. This is a shortnose sawshark.
   It has a nose like a saw.
2. This is a blacktip reef shark.
   It has fins that are black on the tips.
3. This is a Pacific angel shark.
   It has fins that are wide like an angel's wings.
4. This is a hammerhead shark.
   It has a head that looks like the head of a hammer.
5. This is a zebra shark.
   It has stripes like a zebra.
6. This is a frilled shark.
   It has frills on the sides of its head.

Page 113

1. In Shadow Tag, the person who is "It" tries to step on someone's shadow.
2. You need light and something to block the light to make a shadow.
3. The size and shape of a shadow depends on where the sun is in the sky.
4. There can be a shadow at night if there is moonlight or light from a night-light or flashlight.
5. sun, moonlight, night-light, flashlight

1. true
2. false
3. true
4. false

Page 114

block—to keep something from passing through
tag—a children's game
light—the thing that lets us see more easily
bump—to collide with

Sentences will vary.

Page 115

1. shadow   **o**   11. paid   **a**
2. player   **a**   12. strange   **a**
3. space   **a**   13. shine   **i**
4. outside   **i**   14. know   **o**
5. seen   **e**   15. night   **i**
6. light   **i**
7. lower   **o**
8. time   **i**
9. shape   **a**
10. sky   **i**

Order will vary.
1. outside   4. overhead
2. anything   5. bedroom
3. sometimes   6. flashlight

Sentences will vary.

Page 116

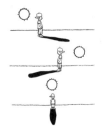

Page 120

1. He hooked a huge catfish and it pulled him into the river.
2. Bill learned the ways of wild creatures. OR Bill learned how to move, hunt, and talk like a wild animal.
3. Hank told Bill that cowboys have fleas and howl at the moon sometimes. Or Hank had Bill look at his reflection in the water to see that he did not have a tail like a coyote.
4. Pecos Bill could ride and rope better than anyone.
5. a. it was very heavy
   b. he had an idea

Cause—A catfish pulled on the fishing line.
Effect—He grew up with a coyote family.

Page 121

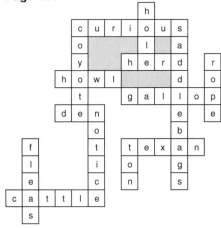

Page 122

~~w~~rong   ~~K~~nee   ta~~l~~ks   si~~g~~n
clim~~b~~   ~~w~~rote   lis~~t~~en   ~~K~~now

1. wrong
2. listen   talks
3. know   sign

rope   nose   sew
boat   hole   bowl

Page 123

1. cowboy   3. saddlebags
2. catfish   4. rattlesnake

Sentences will vary.

1. know   4. through
2. flee   5. sent
3. tail

Page 124

Answers will vary, but could include:
Could happen…
A family could travel west.
A baby could fuss and cry.
A baby could fall out of a wagon.
Someone could ride a horse and rope cattle.
A man could be a great cowboy.
Could not really happen…
A five-day-old baby couldn't hold a fishing line in the water.
A fish in the river couldn't have weighed almost a ton.
A baby wouldn't have four coyote brothers.
A cowboy wouldn't use a rattlesnake for a rope.

1. Bill had been fussing and crying since sunup.
2. You aren't a coyote.
3. You don't see any tail, do you?